International Standard Book Number: 0-9605484-1-6
Library of Congress Catalog Card Number: 89-90876
Copyright © The E. W. Scripps Co.
Printed by The Commercial Appeal, Memphis, Tenn.

FAITH IN MY STAR

A selection of his
own words that showcase
the vision and vitality
of E. W. Scripps

Selected and Edited
By Vance H. Trimble

"I want to fit myself for living in the highest planes of civilization . . . Perhaps you think I am visionary or selfish. I think not altogether so. I still have considerable faith in my star."

—E. W. Scripps

INTRODUCTION

Legend pictures E.W. Scripps a rambunctious, red-whiskered, two-fisted swashbuckler whose flaming brain spewed unorthodox new ideas and philosophies at a mile-a-minute clip, while his sinewy right arm reached out to help the underdog blue-collar worker arise and kick over the plutocrats' silver caviar tray.

All true, but woefully inadequate as a complete portrait; to stop there would be about like savoring the magnificence of the Grand Canyon from a single postcard.

Few people truly knew Scripps in his liftime; even fewer have understood and appreciated him since he entered his ocean grave in 1926. He was a complex, thinking man and an innovator. But he hid out from the world—a hermit who enjoyed holing up at his ranch on a remote rattlesnake mesa where he could savor the ocean and Nature. He wanted to raise a large family—children of his loins (sons to carry on the business) and children of his brain (his little crusading newspapers)—and to read and read and to think and think—and then think some more about the world and its ways.

□ □ □

By no means is this document an attempt to paint a full portrait of the Old Man. It is, rather, a casual, hop-skip glimpse of EWS's personal dynamics.

The vehicle for invading his brilliant mind is the staggering mass of personal writings he carefully preserved and left for posterity—at least 350,000 pages of correspondence, essays, disquisitions, and private "diary notes."

His candor is staggering. He hid no secrets. His is a "kiss and tell" legacy. A less courageous personality might have trashed the documents that detail his bachelor romances, his long struggle with the bottle, his errant fits of depression, and the like. Not Scripps. He kept an honest record of foibles and failures, as well as his towering triumphs.

□ □ □

Charles E. Scripps in 1988 relinquished custody of his grandfather's papers to Ohio University. They are now installed as The Edward Willis Scripps Archive at Alden Library, available as a tremendous research source for scholars exploring the fascinating history of turn-of-the-century American journalism.

In modern times perhaps the only person who has plowed through all of this EWS correspondence is Vance Trimble, retired editor of *The Kentucky Post,* who as a Scripps-Howard Washington correspondent in 1960 won the Pulitzer prize for national reporting. His interest in EWS was sparked in 1980 while editing and updating the third edition of *The Scripps-Howard Handbook.*

Hoping to produce a definitive biography of Scripps, Trimble burrowed into mountainous files. He traveled across the country, as well as to Rome and Shanghai, to view the scenes where major events took place in the Scripps saga, collecting material and interviewing sources.

It took eight years of work, and finally, after much sweat, frustration and rewriting, the book was accepted in January 1989, for publication by The Iowa State University Press.

Considered by Charles Scripps as the foremost "expert" on the life of EWS, Trimble was commissioned by the Scripps Howard Foundation to collect an assortment of Scripps' writings to give a scattered but broad-based insight into EWS's everyday practices and philosophies, and especially his human side.

□ □ □

Again, a caution: These are random excerpts from a mountain of mail, a lifetime of ideas and memories. They are neither complete nor all-encompassing of this singular personality's vital and vibrant mind. Yet you should find them enormously interesting and insightful on the nature of the man's force.

When 18-year-old EWS left the family farm at Rushville, Ill., for his $3-a-week office boy job in Detroit, his sister Ellen (1836-1932), his "second mother," chastised him for writing poor letters home. She complained that he "ignored a thousand and one things desirable to tell and interesting to know . . . Promise to write once a week . . . Long letters . . . Let us have your best thoughts. I think I have a right to them."

He saw her point and complied. From then on it was not a chore, but his fondest ritual. Throughout life he wrote Ellen; virtually a letter a day. The same with sister Annie (1847-1898), his morals preceptor. He turned out hundreds of thousands of letters. His final word count would be no less than one hundred million words—probably more.

Herein, with explanatory notes, are presented some of his writings. Figuring prominently in some of the correspondence are his older half-brothers, James E. (1835-1906) and George H. (1839-1900), his choir-girl wife Nackie (1866-1930), whom he married October 7, 1885, at West Chester, Ohio, his parents, James Mogg Scripps (1803-1873) and Julia (1814-1893), and his first partner Milton McRae (1858-1930).

CONTENTS

DREAMS OF GREATNESS

". . . a literary life"

March 16, 1873

From Detroit to his father:
"You see . . . . I cannot throw away all my ideas, books . . . Had I had my own way I would have chosen . . . a literary life; I might have been a success, that is my reasoning . . . or make myself more thoroughly miserable. As it is I am not quite smart enough to make a passable lunatic."

March, 1875

From Detroit to Annie:
"If I ever do anything it will be simply by making a hit and not pursuing the slow laborious path to eminence. The fact is, I had rather be a nobody than a man of small note."

". . . a little kingdom"

June 24, 1878

In Rome on his 24th birthday, EWS wound up at midnight in the Colosseum, and lay on a hunk of stone, smoking for hours and conning his future. His unpublished autobiography says:
"Everything in and about Rome came to me

1/EWS

with exciting familiarity from my memories of it in books. I dreamed of the emperor who built the Colosseum, and many other emperors, Roman generals and soldier adventurers, and I recalled to mind the names of many great men . . . . Perhaps my choice was an odd one, but it fell on Fabius Maximus; he who was patient and knew how to wait . . . . The world belongs to him who waits, if he doesn't wait too long; if he only waits long enough for his opportunity and then is quick to seize it! . . . As I dreamed I poetized my philosophy and deepened and strengthened my resolve to be one of the great men of the world.

"I saw that I could make use of the story of the Roman Empire.

"I decided that I would extend this kingdom of mine, which would consist of my first newspaper, to another and then another newspaper, and I determined as long as I lived to go on extending my kingdom into perhaps an empire of journalism . . ."

June 29, 1878

From Rome to Annie:

"The chances are 10 million to one that I will never succeed . . . My monument, if it ever rears itself above the low level of a dream, will not stand on the groans of a million fellow human beings . . . . On the contrary I would have it reared aloft not by captive thousands but emancipated generations.

"The day of the sword has passed. The pen is the scepter of this century and will be for ages to come. The press is the engine by which the grand object must be achieved, and the power is now existent, only waiting for the hand of a man wise enough to direct it.

"In a lifetime I may at least start the ball rolling.

"Well, I am a dreamer, am I not? Burn this

2/EWS

letter, and say nothing about its contents."

May 1, 1878

On his first trip abroad, with and at George's expense, EWS comments on night-walking London's streets, in his autobiography:

"I was considering deeply . . . what goal in life I should seek . . . by what road I should arrive at the eminence which I had so long dreamed."

May 17, 1878

In Paris EWS offered a deal to George, as he writes in his autobiography:

"I proposed that when we got home we should go to Cleveland, Ohio, and there start a new paper—an undertaking that would be more venturesome than the founding of *The Detriot Evening News* . . . . He (George) was to furnish the money and leave me alone, and I was to furnish the brains and make us both rich."

. . . back to his Rome "vision"

October 4, 1924

Returning to Rome to try to recapture his "dream of greatness," Scripps writes Ellen:

"It was a policy I have never since deviated from, at least in a general way of speaking. This line of policy was, first, go slow and wait for opportunity. Lay one brick at a time and see it is well cemented in its place. Fight only when I had to fight, and then fight to a finish. Patience was to be my watchword and also persistence.

"It is quite probable had I never gone to London or Paris or Rome I would have sooner or later, quite as determinedly, come to the same conclusion. I would in all probability, have followed the same course."

EWS climbed again to the upper tier of the Colosseum, and found it now different.

"Ellen, it was not impressive. I was disappointed . . . . This time I could not get any thrills in Rome."

His life story ruined

September 17, 1925

EWS assigned his ace Washington correspondent, Gilson Gardner, to edit his autobiography, written in 1915. Gardner tried to sanitize it, and the infuriated EWS wrote Ellen:

"I was surprised and disgusted . . . The foolish fellow thought it was his duty to edit out . . . most everything of a personal character which he was idiot enough to think reflected upon my character and then he transcribed some parts of disquisitions which he considered laudatory . . . .

"I only read a few chapters but a McRae could not have been more boastful than did Gardner make me out to be . . . . Some day my grandchildren may want to read this material . . . . All the labor and expense of this work by Gardner has been wasted."

THE PENNY PAPER IDEA

". . . from my big brother"

1868, Rushville, Ill.

In his unpublished autobiography, EWS explains how his older half-brother, James E. Scripps, planted with him the idea of publishing little four-page newspapers and selling them for as little as a penny. James, a successful editor in Detroit, was visiting the farm home and had one of his rare talks with his then rustic 14-year-old sibling, four years before James was to found *The Detroit Evening News.*

"The idea that my brother submitted to me was the publication of a daily newspaper, very small in size, with large type, and which, by reason of having condensed writing would contain all the news . . . found in the large 'blanket sheets' and sell for two cents or a penny."

No sifting chaff

November 2, 1878

How well EWS adapted the concept is revealed in his salutary on the front page of his first issue of the *Cleveland Penny Press:*

"What the business men want is a newspaper which will present before them all the news of the day in as short and concise a form as possible. They haven't time to spend hours searching thru the length and breadth of a blanket sheet, sifting out much chaff for the few valuable kernels of important news.

"What the laborer and the mechanic wants is to be able to get all the information of the large daily papers at a price he can afford to pay.

"What the ladies want is to be able to keep as well posted as their husbands without having to wade thru columns to obtain information that might be placed in a paragraph.

"What everyone wants is a daily newspaper at a time convenient for reading, containing all the news of the day, containing not one line of uninteresting matter, and cheap enough so that no one will miss the price of it. *The Penny Press.*"

EDITOR & PUBLISHER

". . . a clever paragraph"

January 13, 1878

To Annie:

"I would rather a thousand times be a brilliant writer of no account in a business way than the best editor who ever lived. I like money well enough but it takes a pile of it to make me feel half as well as the consciousness of having written a clever paragraph, or experienced a thought in becoming words."

". . . tell no lies"

November 2, 1878

As editor, EWS announced on page one of the first issue of the *Cleveland Penny Press:*

"We have no politics that is in the sense of the word as commonly used. We are not Republican nor Democratic, nor Greenback, nor Prohibitionist. We simply intend to support good men and condemn bad ones, support good measures and condemn bad ones, no matter what party they belong to.

"We shall tell no lies about persons or policies for love, malice or money. It is no part of a newspaper's business to array itself on the side of this or that party, or fight, lie and wrangle for it.

7/EWS

"The newspapers should simply present all the facts the editor is capable of obtaining, concerning men and measures before the bar of the public, and then, after having discharged its duty as a witness, be satisfied to leave the jury in the case—the public—to find the verdict."

When genius smiles

November 17, 1878

To Ellen:
"The active work of the newspaper office . . . represses all inspiration out of my now active brain. It is no use my trying to ever accomplish literary fame as long as I am employed actively in journalism.

"My genius is a lazy, fickle creature and luxurious. She smiles only when I am happy and when at thorough rest in body and mind. Occasionally at long intervals she peeps in upon me as I sit surrounded by dust and strife, and I long to drop all other thoughts and cling to her but she will not stop. I have to grind out copy and when necessity demands I revenge myself by turning out the dullest of dull copy."

". . . a barrel of ink"

In his autobiography, EWS says in the Cleveland start-up he was "chock full of opinions and ideas that were more the result of emotional activities than reasoning, so having a barrel of ink and plenty of paper, I just turned myself loose on the public."

". . . takes nerve and muscle"

To Annie, EWS gives a blow-by-blow account of how his raw recruits battle Pulitzer's veterans in St. Louis:

"I encounter a thousand petty annoyances of the day—the appeals for favor, the settlement of grievances, the prattle of most fools, the rectifying of grave errors caused not infrequently by my haste in giving orders to the men, etc., etc. ad infinitum.

"The day wears on. I am anxious. A good article comes in. Ha! Have they got it? Is it a scoop? Or have they got it in even better style than my man's? I am eager for the first edition of the rival. It comes. I am either delighted or cast down, according as the tide of merit sets toward them or us.

"I bite my lips and stamp with rage if I find they have done something good which we have not, and woe betide the culprit who is to blame if he meets me then!

"Then I am just as anxious to see the next edition. The *Post-Dispatch* has but two . . . Frequently in their last edition appear their best articles. I am uneasy to see it. The moment the boy fetches it, I seize it, tear over its columns, and let go a sigh of relief or a roof-shaking expletive, as the case may be.

"If the day has been a defeat, I damn everybody all 'round. If it has been a victory, I ask the boys down to take 'suthin' [something]. Thus they know whether they have done their duty like brave men or have been lazy cowards.

"I often come home at night completely worn out with the strain, either miserably blue or languid content. I tell you the life of a newspaperman is a hurly-burly one, and it takes nerve and muscle."

". . . nuggets of gold"

Winter, 1887

From Paris in 1887, James E. Scripps suggests EWS try the Parisien style, not a true newspaper, but printing "nuggets of gold." He tried it four months then revealed his discovery in his *History of The Scripps League:*

"Namely, that Americans want a newspaper and they want news. Their literary education and their refinement is such that it must be confessed they prefer an item of news inelegantly written, even bald or irreverently, to the finest literary work and genius . . . of elegant, brilliant and witty writers."

". . . kicking and flinging"

In his feud with cousin and business partner John Sweeney, and facing trouble in Detroit and Cleveland, EWS wrote Ellen:

". . . After all at the bottom, I know I don't care whether I prevail or fail. It is only the animal instinct that sets me on to fight and peck and use my spurs to the end of ruling my little hen roost in spite of the knowledge that my own neck has to be wrung sooner or later.

"I think that I might give up fussing and fuming except that by coincidence or other reason it seems that whenever I get real mad and desperate enough to start swearing and kicking and flinging things, things do wake up all along the line, with every mule pulling harder the old wagon does creak on farther up the road . . . ."

A kinder newspaper

After settling a mean libel suit for $282, EWS

suddenly developed a new philosophy, writing Ellen:

"Another thing to be considered is the difference between my old methods—which unfortunately are still those of *The Detroit News*—and where the former was to win by fear, while the latter is by favor.

"By my (new) methods of conducting *The Post* I have gained for the newspaper and myself general goodwill and kind feeling. This makes the business more comfortable and I believe more solid. I have been steadily at work pulling *The Cleveland Press* around into the same line, healing up old sores, and making more warm friends for it and its proprietors . . . .

"My idea is to make a good interesting paper that will sell as a foundation. Then for influence, obtain it by solid, sound argument and kindly persuasion instead of by the usual method—old fashioned fierce attacks and exposures.

"The reputation of a bully and cynic or sharper is unprofitable in journalism as in private life. The reputation for bravery, kindheartedness, and honest dealing is just as profitable in journalism as in private life."

Bossing on the rush

October 26, 1888

As president of the Scripps Publishing Company, directing all four of its papers, EWS moved after three years' exile on his honeymoon farm to revitalize *The Detroit News,* writing Ellen:

"I feel so strong and controlling among these poor nervous mortals of the city that I cannot at all times resist the natural spirit of a bully. I am continually surprised, too, at the ease with which so many bend to my push . . . . One thing I do know: I have got things by the nape of the neck and the seat of the pants and on the rush . . . . It is lucky I've done a lot of thinking before . . . so that I am able to decide quickly."

Editors are not clerks!

October 8, 1895

The *St. Louis Chronicle* lost $65,325 in 1895, and EWS hopped McRae:
"You make [Editor-in-chief L.T] Atwood feel that editors are clerks, not to *you only* but also the business manager and advertising men . . . . Demonstrate your confession to the power of editors. If you disagree, write me bluntly . . . . You are wasting valuable years by giving chances to men that in the bottom of your heart you hope will do but you do not expect to do . . . ."

". . . nothing half-told"

November 11, 1895

To George A. Shives at the *St. Louis Chronicle:*

"First, without regard to friendship or enmity, personal qualities to please or antagonize, without pity for individual suffering, men must be placed and displaced, rewarded or the reverse solely on account of the ability or abilities to do *the* thing required in *the* place under consideration.

"The disappointments of my career have been mainly that those I most loved were delinquent and too often that those whom I disliked had to get the good things—*for the good of the papers.*

"Second, ours are news papers rather than opinion-making journals. They are becoming more of the former and less of the latter daily and will eventually have but one mission. There was a time when people bought, read, and studied journals for the purpose of getting ready-made opinions. The power of editors made them arrogant and made them abuse their power to such an extent they lost it almost all.

"Even in my 20 years' experience I have seen the greatest fall of this power, controlling the utterances of our papers read by nearly a million people. I feel that I have less of this power today than I had 16 years ago when *The Press* was my only organ and it had about 12,000 circulation . . . . While people are thus turning from us as guides to opinion they are fairly tumbling over each other in their efforts to buy the sheets of paper which are printed over with facts—information—news on which to found their own opinions . . . .

"Our customers . . . not only want facts (news) but all the news—nothing half-told for effect to fool them and cause them to form false opinions . . . .I think the time has already begun to come when we must be even more careful not to allow men who pay for space (advertisers) to lie too strongly.

"The third point . . . . We are running newspapers not advertising sheets. We are to make money by making newspapers that will sell and because they will sell will be patronized by advertisers."

Fire him—or I will!

To Milton McRae (on straightening out Will Kellogg [a second-cousin by marriage] at the *Kansas City World* for gossiping about the family):

"If you don't either discharge Kellogg or shut him up, I will come home and do it myself. Sometimes I feel that you yourself dislike to admit to your subordinates that I (and not the Scripps-McRae League) am supreme . . . . Obey my orders as you expect your orders to be obeyed."

The double disaster

In November 1898, EWS bought the *San Francisco Report* and hired a red-headed Cincinnati sports writer named George Gohen as editor at an astounding $75 a week, even though Gohen had a bad drinking problem. EWS caught flak from his own troops, but snapped back at Milton McRae:

"Please drop the Gohen matter for the present. Gohen is not the only man who has won my high favor and esteem much to the surprise of other people . . . . Perhaps I have at this time given him double the salary that Taft *[the Times-Star]* gave him . . . . I never regulated your salary or that of any other man by the market price, but solely by the worth of the man . . . .

"It pays to pay a good man more than he can demand. Don't forget that although I do make mistakes in weighing men, I have also made some happy choices . . . . I don't think I ever desecrated the office of editorship with a lightly considered appointment. Gohen's faults have made him an easy mark for competitors in the race for office.

"The same judgment that has prompted my dealings with you and many another man leads me to predict that Gohen will yet be a wealthy, prominent and honorable man. I feel that he is of good enough stuff to be entitled to my most earnest efforts in his behalf.

"Given a man of Gohen's energy, assisted by a man of experience . . . . some persimmons would likely be shaken from the tree."

Gohen and the *Report* were twin-disasters, perhaps EWS's worst newspapering calamity. The paper failed in a few months. Later Gohen tried to blackmail the concern with gossip about George Scripps and maids at Miramar, but failed.

December 6, 1898

On arrival in San Francisco, Gohen got this letter from the Old Man:

"Remember you are beginning a new career—that of tight-fisted, cautious, money-making man.

"The outward mein of such a man is one that indicated self-confidence and perfect assurance, but deep down inside of him such a man is so doubtful of himself that he never takes chances . . . . I have only one serious fear for you, and that you know of.

[EW meant boozing. He bet $200 Gohen couldn't stay on the wagon three months. Gohen won.]

January 19, 1899

To Gohen:

"It was with no desire to hurt your feelings or wound your *amour propre* that I told you I count altogether on your personal force, your loyalty and intelligence in obeying my orders in the beginning and not upon your business judgment or even your journalistic judgment in business.

"The foundation on which Scripps newspapers were successfully built was not low price, not high literary skill, not artistic typography, not fine paper, nor a large amount of reading matter.

"It was founded on the correct appreciation of the fact that very industrious men had small time to read papers and that indolent people—and also the great majority of people—are not fond of reading, hence we founded our papers on the theory that nearly everybody wanted to know what was happening—that nearly everybody was a lover of gossip—that they wanted to learn these things with as little labor as possible.

"In fact we started with the hypothesis that a four-line paragraph, no matter how incomplete or how grammatical, or how badly worded, announcing the news fact would sell newspapers better than the most elaborate, most complete and most elegant article that could be produced by the brightest minds.

"You well know that most of our papers have wandered very far from this principle and that they have still continued to succeed but you cannot know that the main reason for this success has been that we have not had as competitors men who knew the secret that we did . . . .

"Another principle has been in (the) case of our very successful properties that we did not run our papers for fun but for profit, and that we never made an effort to win public favor by false pretenses and show.

"I don't care a damn what other newspaper men or publishers are thinking or doing in San Francisco. I propose that the *Report* shall be the smallest possible paper, only large enough to hold a brief mention of all the important news facts, and I propose that it shall save money in every particular except three: first, that of getting news quickly; second, that of printing it promptly; and, third, that of so managing its circulation department as to enable every would-be buyer possible to buy."

Fights NEA rebuff

August 22, 1902

EWS was appalled his editors tried to snub and low rate the output of his Newspaper Enterprise Association syndicate (NEA)—editorials and features alike. To E.H. Wells at the *Seattle Star:*

"I want to tell you that you made an awful bad break on the NEA matter. What you said about NEA you said about E.W. Scripps, for NEA is E. W. Scripps, and it was created for just the opposite purpose you supposed it was. Whatever you do, I expect you to hereafter be loyal to this enterprise . . . ."

Blue-collar mouthpiece

March 21, 1903

In launching on this date the *San Francisco News,* EWS advised the editor, W.D. Wasson, to be the working man's friend—"the mouthpiece for those who have no other mouthpiece . . . . Hook yourself tight to the heart of the common people. Be always with and of them . . . .

"If we can prove that it is possible to publish in San Francisco a daily newspaper that is almost reckless in its daring, in its loyalty to the common people, and defiant of the aristocratic masses, we will have set on foot the work of the emancipation of the press of this country.

"We will prove that newspapers can be owned and run by people who are not millionaires, and . . . without any sort of subsidy [advertising] from the millionaire classes."

"Your paper is dull"

April 28, 1903

EWS let a former secretary, George Putnam, start the *Spokane Press,* but scolded him:

"Your paper is dull. Your staff is spreading itself too thin . . . . All any paper needs is one column of news the public must have . . . every day." [Putnam couldn't take it, resigning in a few weeks.]

"Don't be afraid"

Sending William Strandborg to the *Seattle Star* as new editor, EWS advised:

"Be yourself . . . hard, and definitive, and pervasive. Make a paper that everybody will read and at the same time be a certificate of your character as a gentleman . . . . Do what [the other papers] are not doing . . . . so that all people will take the *Star* to know what is going on. Don't be too correct. Don't be afraid of making mistakes.

"Don't be afraid of trying experiments. Whatever you feel right hard about, that do . . . . Better an enthusiastic damn fool than perfectly correct and prosy . . . .

"Don't be afraid to act promptly in dealing with your staff . . . . If you have a bad man, let him go. If you don't trust a man, let him go . . . . Don't permit anyone—myself or the president of your company—to persuade you to employ a man you don't want, or discharge a man you think you can make good use of."

". . . mitigate the unwisdom"

May 24, 1922

Addressing the annual conference of his editors in Washington, D. C., Scripps said:

"You are not only to be the advocates of the plain common people, the common people, the 95 percent, but you must give to the ignorant knowledge, and, at least, mitigate the unwisdom of the unwise. So far as the Ten Commandments are applicable to the profession of journalism, they should be observed.

"The most unfortunate situation in regard to journalism is that it is impossible for a journal to be a true servant of the people without its becoming a great property, reckoned by dollars. It is unfortunate that a journalist cannot be at one and the same time a journalist and a St. Francis of Assisi.

"Great journalism has to be an identical twin —a Siamese twin to great wealth."

REPORTERS & PRINTERS

Write in blood

September 9, 1880

To his brother James:

"I want characteristic men writing [for the *Chronicle*]—men who when they write dip their pens into the gall of their heart's blood and not into the colorless saliva that drivels from their mouths . . . I learned that success did not so much lay in having *everything* in the paper as having everything that was in the paper *good*.

"I would rather my reader before opening my paper feel certain he was going to be entertained than that he was going to be instructed."

"Plunged into . . . the blues!"

March 12, 1881

Leaving the *St. Louis Chronicle* in other hands, EWS going back to Cleveland tells Annie:

"My health is broken. My spirits are depressed. My weakness is confessed . . . . I have lost a great deal of money here [Chronicle lost $18,600; Press made $12,600]. I fear for my sanity. Aye, I am plunged into the deepest of the fearful abyss, the blues!"

"Would . . . murder for me"

From St. Louis, to Annie:

"Suspicion, slander and treachery turn up everywhere." EW reported that only one poor little employee that "I saved in Cincinnati and sent over here is really loyal to me, and he is too loyal. He would lie, steal, or murder for me!'

"It is hard for me to understand myself. I find myself so often in the same day feared, hated, or held in contempt—and loved, respected, and admired . . . . I certainly have the gift for waking other people's passions in the most astounding way."

"Bold leaders"

To Annie:

"Little by little, I am drawing closer to my men here. I think some have hearts I can capture. Men usually like bold and reckless leaders, and they warm to me. I see a faint streak of light and I may yet steer to the enchanted island whose caves hold my half-million gold."

A pay raise

April 25, 1881

EWS instructs *Cleveland Press* Foreman Crockett to give printers 10 percent pay raises:

"The *Penny Press* is now making a fair profit, and its proprietors are pleased to be able in this way to express their kind regards for men whom they consider personal friends as well as employees.

"Appreciating the high state of morality that prevails among The *Press* printers we feel no doubt that this increase of wages will be spent in no foolish way but will contribute to the comfort of wives and babies, present and future."

Free to write

Winter, 1878

From the first in Cleveland, EWS says in his *The History of The Concern*, he gave his reporters free rein:

"Each member of the staff was allowed to produce about whatever copy he wanted to. My business was to select what I wanted to print; and my editing of the copy consisted of simply cutting it down to occupy the least space. I soon left this work to someone else." In his autobiography he said: "I considered my main role was to make an important decision about every six months."

"The first throat to be cut"

Union printers, disgruntled by the advent of the Linotype, decided to start their own paper in Cincinnati. Scripps warned they would fail and pointed out for every printer let go, two new men had to be hired as a result of the growth of the business. He wrote Ellen:

"Frank Rist [the union spokesman] knew I was recognized as one of the best and fairest employers in the country yet he pleaded our machines had thrown out a lot of men, but admitted we had employed more men in other lines than before.

"George told me that if the revolution came I would have to suffer with the rich, and I admitted it . . . . Mine will be the first throat to be cut . . . . Printers are out of work and their families are suffering and hence they are deaf to logic and appeals for justice . . . ." [Scripps was correct; the printers' paper folded after 33 days.]

A CHARMED LIFE

". . . faith in my star"

On his 27th birthday, EWS proposes to Ellen they travel abroad:

"I am densely ignorant of all things outside the narrow limits of my obscure life. I want to travel and learn what I can from observation . . . to become acquainted with people and places . . . to learn at least the French and German languages.

"I want to enter into a course of historical study that will amuse as well as instruct . . . I want to read up on modern and ancient theology and philosophy . . . and the principal schools of modern philosophy. I want to become proficient in the sciences of government.

"In light literature I want to become acquainted with all the great works of German, French and English nations . . . I want to enjoy art, both painter and sculptor, the architect, the musician. I can never be more than an understanding observer of such works, but I want to be at least that. I want to fit myself for living in the highest planes of civilization . . . .

"Perhaps you think I am visionary or selfish. I think not altogether so. I still have considerable faith in my star."

". . . dig for money"

To Ellen:

"I am doing pretty well at present, but you must not expect too much of me . . . . You will have to be satisfied if I succeed in stopping just short of physical and moral self-destruction . . . .

"I think I may yet make a tolerably fair figure during my life . . . . I have made one of those pledges to myself that I will never break—that for three years more I will dig for money and at the end return to a secluded and calm life . . . .

"I may marry but that is now hardly probable. If I do not, I want to go way off from all the places and people I have known during these years of ambition, and build myself a home where I can live in peace and obscurity and spend my more restless energies in travel.

"That may be the only way I can save myself from being what you fear, a boozy imbecile. Despite your and Annie's delicate pleadings to save myself, I seem to lead a charmed life. I was born to fill a grander mission than most men . . . . My two great dangers are financial ruin and the whiskey bottle. I can only hope to escape them . . . .

"I wonder if I am to be pursued all my life by the hellish demon of ambition armed with a whip of snakes."

"I have pretty eyes"

1884

Writes Ellen about his sexy charm winning a libel case:

"I have demonstrated once again to my satisfaction that I am a better lawyer than these bigwigs that I have to hire. But this time I had to practice wheelings [sic] instead of bulldozings.

"You know I have pretty eyes and, when properly regulated, a very moaning tone of voice. I know I should not have succeeded had I not brought both of these to bear on the wife of the complainant. Said wife being pretty good looking aided me in my inspirations. I believe I could get the woman to kiss me for my mother.

"As it was she only shed a few tears of sympathy for me and told her husband to take $500 and let me go. Ain't I ashamed of myself."

". . . vice of laziness"

July 26, 1883

After a physical for a $100,000 life insurance policy, EWS tells Ellen he realizes he is "the only healthy member of my family.

"Is this because my vice of laziness has caused me to rest often and easy? Because I have checked my nervousness with nicotine, and because by use of stimulants I have forced out of my system all sloughs and disease-breeding germs?

"If my life and habits, despite being in violation of the rules laid down by old women and some doctors are not the causes of my present condition, why is it that so many people who started with good constitutions against my bad one and went to bed early and got up early, took light suppers, eschewed tobacco, drank no spirits, worked regularly and systematically recreated and who have obeyed all the other rules of healthy conduct have turned out such wrecks?"

Saving old letters

June 1, 1900

After George's death, attorneys tried to find correspondence nailing down his residence city for an on-going fight over his will. To his lawyer J.C. Harper, Scripps wrote:

"Ellen asked me to destroy certain portions of letters referring to the family. I told her I would not do so . . . . It is not my habit to destroy letters . . . . Every letter received by me in the last 20 years is in existence, mainly at Miramar."

". . . not dying of dry rot"

At age 62, EWS writes editor C.D. Wheeler:
"I went under the harrow when I was barely 19.
I have worked myself out completely. All I want to
do now is read and read . . . . I have had a brimful
life; I have had lots of fun; I have not done many
things I am ashamed of . . . . I am not dying of dry
rot; I am never bored; I meet few people, but quite
enough . . . . I am not yearning to get back to the
firing line."

". . . broken-hearted portrait"

August 22, 1922

The portrait of EWS that hangs in the board-
room at Scripps Howard's headquarters in Cincinnati was painted by John Young-Hunter. Over the
years, it has become the most frequently repro-
duced image of Scripps Howard's founding father.
However, EWS didn't like the portrait, and told
Ellen so:

"I am almost a perfect stranger to myself.
Gilson Gardner and others on the boat declared the
portrait to be an excellent one. He certainly did
make me look like a broken-hearted old man, but he
has just as certainly represented me as a fat and

quite aged man, and then too he has accentuated my nose."

. . . First novel "butchered"

After composing a novel, his first, called "Theory and Practice," he writes Ellen:

"This morning I read over several pages of the novel that I wrote while I was on Long Island Sound, but it greatly disappointed me. I am sure as bad as my book might have been, the stenographer butchered it.

"I found it easy and very amusing to compose my first story. Whether it is good or bad, it poured out of me in a perfect stream, and I imagine that was partly the trouble with the stenographer. I know I was 30 hours altogether on the book, and calculating by counting the words, I think it would be a 400-page novel."

DRINKING & SMOKING

"In vino veritas"

Mike Dee, city editor of *The Detroit Evening News*, lectured 21-year-old cub reporter EWS on handling booze, as Scripps recounted in his *History of The Scripps League*:

"Mike explained the necessity of being mildly bibulous and of not being too bibulous . . . . It was my duty to be very crafty in my behavior at the bar . . . . Take advantage of my companion by stealthily spilling on the floor the greatest part of my drinks. He even quotes Latin to me . . . *In vino veritas* — Get our man drunk and he tells the truth."

1877, Detroit

In his autobiography:

"I never smoked before breakfast . . . but from the time I had eaten my morning meal until I lay down at night to sleep, the only time I was not smoking was when I was eating my meals or attending a theater, church, or some social event . . . . I quit attending church because I could not smoke there."

"No one knows"

July 27, 1884

To Annie:

"My own careless talk has led to a very general opinion that I am considerable of a drunkard. I drink on the European plan and while in a year's time I may consume more liquor than most men, I take it in such a way and at such times that except for the few friends who drink with me, no one knows of my drinking at all, unless I speak of it."

". . . a fit of horrors"

Spring, 1898

After Milton McRae and Bob Paine came to Miramar sometime between February and May in 1898 for a business conference, EWS put this typed memo in his file:

"I had a fit of horrors, went into hysterics and swore and cussed and raged like a fool. There it is; when I am well I can feel so confident. Directly I get sick. I am as bad as a woman and worse than a baby. I'm disgusted with myself.

"Paine and McRae enjoyed their visit. I did not drink much while they were here, but after they left I did drink a great deal. I had tuned up to a high key to do things and there was nothing to do.

"I might as well kill myself with business as with whiskey, and I might as well kill myself with whiskey as with business.

"Years ago I gave myself 40 years of life, and lived at that pace. It is my misfortune that my physical condition has proved to be superior to my plans.

"For about 10 weeks I have been employed in the miserable task of attending to details and raising money. The task is too great for me. I can't endure it. Impossible for me to do anything halfway. I must be exercising all my judgment, or doing nothing."

". . . made a hard fight"

August 27, 1898

To Ellen:
"My health is better. I have made a hard fight against alcohol and nicotine. Wrote today and smoked and drank. The result will be a setback. I am between the devil and the deep sea. If I have nothing to do, I stimulate; if I have much to do, I stimulate."

". . . a gallon a day"

In his autobiography, written in 1915, Scripps makes an astounding claim on tippling that no medical doctor would accept as fact:

"During these busy years . . . one thing distressed me more than anything else—my fixed habit of drinking . . . . While I was never really intoxicated more than a half-dozen times in my life, perhaps, and while I was not many more times even in the least befuddled or over-exhilarated, I consumed enormous quantities of alcohol.

"I could drink enough whiskey in one day—without having my brain clouded in the least—to keep four or five ordinary men drunk for a week.

"I have never known, or known of, another man who could drink a gallon of whiskey a day—as was my custom for a long time—and at the same time do business or carry on any professional work, and those whose life was not quickly extinguished . . . . Later I did reduce my tippling from four quarts a day to two quarts a day."

Eyesight failing

May 17, 1899

To Ellen:

"I suppose you have heard that I have engaged

a physician to travel with me this summer. I have turned myself over to him in most respects. He is watching me rather carefully as to diet. He also has got me keeping better hours. As for my nervous condition, I feel much improved . . . . I can go all day in a stormy meeting without fatigue.

"In St. Louis I saw an oculist who said he could not do anything for me as my eyes were failing me on account of the condition of my nerves. He said if I would quit smoking and drinking I might have better eyesight some day.

"A great deal of satisfaction in that, isn't there? I'm quite temperate—but not quite yet, by a long ways.

"I have given up using my good eye and am using the blind eye in the little work I have to do such as signing checks and documents, etc."

LOVE & MARRIAGE

". . . I feel happier"

September 23, 1888

To Ellen:
"Perhaps you mistake the date of this letter and think that it was written three days instead of three years after my marriage but I am 34 years old and the father of a family.

"There are times when I feel happier and more in love than ever a bridegroom could be. This beautiful day in the last part of September is one of the times when life is worth a good deal more than living to me."

". . . almost feel warm lips"

June 17, 1893

While waiting at Miramar for his mother to die, he writes his wife Nackie:
"Yesterday afternoon I started for the seashore; passed the station, passed the point where the rattler made Benito jump, passed (after stopping for glass of orange phosphate) the little Sorrento store, around the south hills to the stone ridge, passed on and on until I came to a delightful little cove about half a mile south of Del Mar—a beautiful little cove where two lovers might hide away

from all view with only the blue sea rolling away westward to meet the cool breeze coming eastward; with only the sun above to see.

" 'Tis a beautiful spot and one I shall long remember for the sake of association.

"There in this little cove I sat down on the stones to dream awhile looking far out over the blue westward while my mind's eye wandered back east where my heart is—where my home is, and all my loved ones are.

"In my fancy I could almost feel warm lips pressing mine—could almost hear the sigh of love's contentment.

"But I thought of the black mare, too, and many other things just to see if the picture would change, just to feel love outweigh old resentment. I laughed out loud at myself for even thinking that I was really angry with you.

"What a self-revelation is a time like this to me. You are away. I cannot have you if I will. So I can see now all plainly enough how stupid, how idiotic I am for some little vexation . . . . If no other man ever did feel it, I feel now that one's wife is one's self—not only one-half—but all of one's self. My wife and my babies—my babies and my wife— food and drink, air to breathe—life itself.

"How have I been blessed! No man deserved less and no man has greater love treasure than I have.

"If you were not so awfully practical, so awfully maternal—and I would not have you changed a hair's breadth—you would know just what a slave you have and just what worship he gives you . . . . I have found that I can carry happiness with me only in carrying with me thoughts of you."

". . . an artificial husband"

July 3, 1895

To Ellen:

"I expect to die before my wife, and expect and want her to marry again and am more anxious that she should wait long enough to make a good selection than to preserve appearances. Would I marry again? I am what you call a natural bachelor and an artificial husband."

". . an animal man"

September 1, 1896

To Ellen:

"Nackie seems more beautiful and more powerful over me than ever before in her life, and I am glad of it. I had rather be an animal man than an intellectual giant . . . ."

How Nackie saves!

His wife showed EWS the lighter side of a financial pinch. At an expense down-hold conference in Cincinnati, he wrote Ellen:

"At the hotel I met Nackie. I had a long face and felt like crying. Nackie reflected in her looks the same condition. She agreed to help me in my struggle . . . .

"After a long night's sleep, I sent for the business people. Nackie went out and after a while I began to be disturbed by bellboys running in with packages. They came by the dozen and filled the room with packages.

"Later when Nackie came in, I reproached her for her expenditures. How did she defend herself? 'Why, Ed, you are poor and we have to begin economizing, so I wanted to get everything we needed before. Now don't you think your wife has got some foresight?' "

"If you yearn . . ."

After Scripps suffered a slight stroke, doctors kept his wife away, fearing their quarrels could bring on a fatal seizure. She begged to join him on his yacht. He wrote her:

"Your letters affected me deeply . . . . I have been constantly tempted to be heedless of Dr. Morgan's warning and to not only run the risk of death but to face it and succumb to it as a result of your being with me . . .

"Don't come as long as you would criticize me . . . . You must assume that I have absolute right on my side and neither my children nor you have any right to oppose me or criticize me . . . . If you yearn as much for my companionship, there is no effort you would not make to comply with all the conditions . . . ."

THE RICH & THE POOR

". . . contempt for upper class"

EWS reasoned the *Penny Press* could at least "lift the dense ignorance" that blinded Cleveland's workers to their concentrated political might, to their opportunity to unite for a fairer share of the profits of the factories. His autobiography explains:

"In my youthful conceit I felt a great contempt for those who called themselves the better class. It was obvious that they were satisfied with conditions as they were and had no great inspiration to bring about any change in the social order. I had the conviction that necessity alone would cause the amendment of the manners and the custom of the employer and the ruling class. Not only the propensity but the bare existence of the upper classes depended upon the labor of their employees—the contented productive labor of these people.

"I proposed to do what I could to instruct and educate the workers; to promote the greatest possible discontent on their part with things as they were; to help them in strikes; to encourage them to vote against candidates for office who were careless of their interests, and for candidates who made the greatest concessions to them.

"Trade unionism in those days was weak. I never failed to recognize the faults of trade unionism. But I felt that through it I could exercise a comparatively great influence. Whenever there has been a contest between the ruling classes on one side and the wage-earners on the other, I have chosen to be the friend, associate and fellow-striver of the second party.

"I have assumed that there were enough other forces and other newspapers arrayed against us to insure that no general and far-reaching injustice will result even from the temporary success of men and measures in my party that are bad. It has been my effort to make it harder for the rich to grow richer and easier for the poor to keep from growing poorer."

The 95 percent

April 6, 1909

In his disquisition *Damned Old Crank,* EWS said:

"I am one of the few newspaper men who happen to know that this country is populated by 95 percent of plain . . . and poor . . . people and that [their] patronage is worth more to a newspaper owner than the patronage of the wealthy 5 percent. So I have always run my business along the line of least resistance and for the greatest profit, and . . . I have made money easier than any newspaper publisher did make it . . . .

". . . wealthy damned thieves"

With World War I threatening, EWS thought the blue-collar class was hit hard on taxes, with millionaires getting off light. He growled to his San Diego editor:

"The wealthy people of the United States are damned thieves, or else Congress has been incapable . . . . The rascality of the rich man has been used to influence Congress to rig the tax law with purposeful defectiveness to provide loopholes for the wealthy.

"My own millionaire class could more easily pay a 25 percent income tax than the 99 million common working men could pay 2 to 4 percent. [He was incensed by the short-sightedness of the Treasury Department and its "little $1,800 clerks."]

"The officials are not dishonest, but they are all ignorant on many important facts, and have no capacity for perspective." [The 1914 income tax yielded only $8 million; Scripps said it could have brought in at least $1 billion.]

Service over profits

July 5, 1919

In "retirement," Scripps was not asked to attend the annual conference of his editors, and sent them a chiding letter.

"I heard only briefly from Bob of your discussions, but I believe I am warranted in supposing you have devoted your energies almost wholly to the subject of how to increase the values and profits of our business as a business . . . .

"I recognize that this reproachful letter is based almost exclusively on my knowledge of human nature . . . . We can well afford to dispense with a large part of our wealth and future profits in a way of devoting ourselves and our energies to a great degree of public service."

IN POLITICAL LIFE

Louis XIV's leaf

January 24, 1908

To Bob Paine:

"If some great cataclysm should occur which would put in my hands the power to name the next President and to outline a governmental policy, I would not make a move because I would not know what was best to do.

"I have no other motive for activity than instinct, which impels me to keep moving. I feel like the fellow who bawled into the phonograph receiver: 'I don't know where I'm going, but I'm on my way.'

"No political party is worth my entire respect and confidence. The people as a whole have a right to . . . and power to remedy the glaring faults of the present. I believe they are waiting only for some great moral explosion to lead and crystalize them into action . . . .

"Through my newspapers I intend to do all I can to promote the coming revolution. I do not believe socialism can or should succeed class rule. I do feel that real democracy, at least in the United States, is now possible and practical.

"Louis XIV of France destroyed the aristocracy of his times to the advantage of monarchy by ruining his nobles.

"I am not enough of an original man, or inventor, or statesman to strike off any entirely new idea. The most I am able to do is take a leaf out of history and adopt it, and the leaf I have chosen has been this scheme of Louis XIV's, and for that reason I think it may be best for democracy to ruin the ruling classes in order to construct a sound foundation on which to stand.

"In a vague and perhaps obscure way I have defined my position by declaring myself the antagonist of the 5 percent of the people of this country who at present hold in their grasp 95 per cent of all things material and immaterial which belong to the whole 100 percent of the people.

"Men of great wealth are enemies of the public. . . . . The laws are bad because they have been framed not by the people and for the people, but by the few and for the few."

Cave of Abdullam

Working with Lincoln Steffens, Scripps pushed the common man's "war" on plutocratic oligarchy, inviting to Miramar rich or talented "fighting" insurgents—such as Senator Robert M. LaFollette, Rudolph Spreckels, Louis Brandeis, George Foster Peabody, Gifford Pinchot, Professor Thorstein Veblen, and their like. EWS wrote to Steffens:

"It is proposed to form a combination of patriotic citizens of national repute—men who in one form or another provided their willingness to devote a great part of their time and energy, and some part of their fortune, to the furtherance of the cause of good government, either of municipalities, states, or of the nation—with no regard being paid to the matter of past or present party affiliations."

[The bold scheme for this off-the-record "Cave of Abdullam," at the ranch at Scripps's expense, fizzled after months of struggle, chiefly because no suitable date could be found when all these busy men could drop their tasks and come to Miramar.]

". . . for good or evil"

September 6, 1909

To Lincoln Steffens:
"I must drop out altogether in a few years, and I must leave in the hands of others the power for good or evil that I have created. My successors must inherit the brute force inherent in my institution, but they can no more inherit the spirit that gave it existence than can the tall ship's mast inherit the life-giving sap of the fir tree in the forest."

A Progressive sweep?

December 28, 1909

To Editor W.H. Porterfield:
"Most of the strong men and all of the organizing ability are to be found among those who are called Republicans now. All the really popular men in the dominant party are today out of power. Is it not time for the 'Progessives' to organize?

"Would not the Progressive Party headed by

Roosevelt carry with it all the really liberal and patriotic element of the Republican Party and all the Democrats, except the mossbacks and the millionaires, and easily sweep the country at large and most of the states?

"I am more profoundly interested today than I have ever been in my life in the politico-economic situation in the country."

Don't stay neutral

November 15, 1909

In a mayoralty recall in Los Angeles, son John Paul instructed the *Record* to stay neutral, but father overruled the boy, telling Editor K.J. Murdock:

"I believe it would be impossible for me to ever advise neutrality in any public matter where the people's interests were at stake . . . . There is nothing for the *Record* to do except act in the most effective manner possible so that the anti-machine candidate at the final election shall win . . . .

"If the *Record* people consider this a bitter pill to swallow it is only because they are possessed of human passions, desiring revenge and fearing ridicule. . . ."

". . . must be great change"

EWS made clear to his editors he was willing to support Socialist Eugene Debs for President, writing son John Paul:

"It is not that the cause of socialism has advanced so much, as the fact that the two old parties and the whole political system have fallen so rapidly in public esteem, that makes radicalism so perfectly safe these days. I do not believe we would lose a dollar of income by coming out flat-footed for socialism. I suspect on the other hand we would gain a great deal of income . . .

"It is not up to our newspapers to reform the world. The world is reforming itself. Change in conditions has been in all times, is now, and always will be inevitable.

"It is inevitable that there must be great change in the economic conditions existing in all civilized society. It is not our business to bring about these changes. It is our business, however, to recognize the inevitable change, to take part in it, and be a part of it.

"We must keep our ears and our eyes wide open, and articulate and visualize that which the inarticulate and the more or less blind population only feel. We must help this populace formulate what it feels and visualize what it knows to exist but cannot yet see.

"The time is coming rapidly perhaps when the rule of men of our ideas is to cease. Why should the people select as our successors the men that we approve of, or even of those whom we approve of more than, say, Debs?

"We are part of this present system, and we are a very important part of it. Hence we stand in the way of the change that is inevitable. We must be swept out of existence, or change ourselves and adapt ourselves to the new order of things. There will be not in my lifetime, and perhaps not in your lifetime, anything remotely approaching the ideal of socialism. Thus our lives may be, and probably will be, spent in the enjoyment of those special privileges of ours.

"We do not want to thrust power into the people's hands. The most we want to do is rejoice while we are aiding the people to grab the power. As journalists it is our duty and privilege to submit ourselves to be an organ and an instrument in the hands of the people when they are fit to have it accomplished.

"We are not working for glory, personal and peculiar to ourselves; if we were we would certainly fail. We are working for the race that knows little of us now, and will have forgotten our existence long before they can feel much gain from the service we will have performed.

"Not only financially, but in all other ways, my life has been for the most part fortunate. I have turned over to my sons not only a considerable fortune, but an opportunity such as few young men have ever enjoyed.

"I am almost sure that no matter what else happens, the wealth of every individual among my children will be far greater than my own personal wealth has been, and I am almost equally sure that my children will make excellent use of the opportunities that are a hundredfold greater worth than the wealth that they will have or may derive from me."

An idea for Wilson

EWS felt Woodrow Wilson was unable to deal effectively with the press. He proposed the President should add to his cabinet a "Secretary of the People"—a skilled and respected journalist to be a useful information conduit between White House and the press. He was called to the President's office to air his views, telling Ellen:

"For the first time in my life, I believe, I was stumped and embarrassed, and sat there like a ninny for a moment or two until the President started to talk; but we were only a minute getting to the subject I knew he wanted to talk about.

"Wilson conceded his academic background had proved a handicap. He stated he felt the public's attitude had always been affected by this feeling of distrust of a college president.

"The President confessed he recognized the deficiencies of his administration. He regretted that the official pressures had been so great on him that he had not been able to get out amongst the people and talk to them and meet them face to face. He complained that the pressure on his time was so great he had to do 'his thinking on the run.'

"Wilson was quite enthusiastic about the idea of having a journalistic representative. We discussed the names of several candidates . . . and left the idea to be further discussed with the Cabinet. I suggested they send an envoy to Miramar if the White House wanted my assistance in trying to find the right man for the job.

" . . . Getting somewhat carried away I volunteered that Wilson was probably our greatest President since Lincoln, and told him that perhaps Lincoln's paramount good fortune had been that those around him were successful in making him known to the public more as a human being than as a superman."

"Hold my tongue and look wise"

April 2, 1915

Wilson was silent on the "Secretary of the People" idea for nine months, then sent Secretary of the Interior Franklin W. Lane to Miramar to ask EWS to personally take the job. EWS wrote Bob Paine:

"I was amused and shocked by Lane's suggestion that I myself should go to Washington. Rumor, working at a long distance, had credited me with qualities a thousand times magnified, and some that did not exist . . . .

"Wilson thinks I am a much greater man than I really am. The only way to not shatter the reputation that others had made for me was to hold my tongue and look wise. But I could not do that."

". . . rotten weak spots"

To Bob Paine, EWS suggested Negley Cochran might be a good "Secretary of the People:"

"Can Neg do any good? I don't know. I have no interest in making Wilson's name great in history. At my age . . . there is only one thing worthwhile for me, and that is to help the right men do the right things . . . . I felt at one time that old Roosevelt had it in him to perform tremendous social service. I even now know that he had that power, although it was offset by a selfish egotism that finally prevailed.

"Looking Mr. Wilson in the face, recognizing the tone of complete candor, and even a sort of pained humbleness, as one who is striving mightily to help his own inadequacy, I felt the urge to help.

"I know as a matter of course there are rotten weak spots and yellow streaks in Wilson, just as there are the same things in you and me and everybody else; but I think he fights harder against evil tendencies than you or I do—harder than most men I have known.

"Would it not be possible, if Neg could get under the President's skin, as it were, and be a real tough, though unoffical member of this Cabinet, for him to get Wilson to make some . . . very fine strokes . . . ?"

Pay as we go war

April 2, 1917

EWS badgered Wilson to hunt down German U-boats and to soak the rich on taxes, and make public all income tax returns. He wired Wilson:

"I strongly urge that we should pay as we go in the war with income and inheritance taxes. All income over one hundred thousand dollars should be conscripted. The minimun cash pay for soldiers and sailors should not be less than three dollars a day during the war. Such legislation would cost me more than half my present income."

Private Scripps?

April 5, 1917

EWS sends Secretary of War Newton D. Baker a night letter from Miramar:

"I am 63 years old. Have had no military experience. I am wealthy and at leisure. Have had very large executive experience and have in this state of California a very large number of capable well-trained business men subject to my order. Can you make use of my services? If so I offer them."

ONE-MAN POWER

"I don't ask anybody"

April 22, 1905

Retiring as chairman, Scripps gave the title to Milton McRae, but explained to Bob Paine:

"Dad is going to run Scripps-McRae business in his own way, while he (Dad) is on earth . . . . The kind of advice I want from my cabinet and others is how to do what I want to do. I don't ask anybody to tell me what I should do. I have decided what to do.

"All I want to know is the best way to do it."

". . . a man, not a monkey"

March 29-30, 1905

In five years as president, McRae failed in his cardinal obligation, making 15 percent profit, Scripps laments to Bob Paine:

"He did give me half a loaf and eked it out with a fish—the great volume of business, great national reputation and prestige, etc., which I loathe . . . .

"From his days as general manager, McRae kept hollering at me that he was a man and not a monkey . . . . Now Mac has had his fling . . . . Still he wants to run the whole thing . . . . in fact to be my guardian and keeper of all my possessions."

". . . trouble with Mac"

After a quarrel with McRae over the *St. Louis Chronicle,* EWS complains to Bob Paine:

"Nackie was hurt in a fall from my buckboard, and hasn't fully recovered . . . . I am worried, can't sleep, and am dictating this at midnight . . . .

"It is clear I am going to have trouble with Mac. I may fire him. I may fight him. I may even smash him. I may lose Toledo and Columbus. I have made up my mind to cease wasting time on men who have lost faith in me."

Coveting my power

McRae hated St. Louis, but EWS issued a stern ultimatum: "I do pre-emptorially insist that you live in St. Louis until the newspaper succeeds. All your other duties are eliminated . . . .

"I study more, think more, and analyze more . . . . You act more, and more strenuously . . . . Your pride made you rebel against this relationship of superior and inferior, and caused you to covet my natural position of that power to direct . . . .

"Every man wants a position at the top. I have got it, and I am going to keep it, and you know it . . . ."

Mac's failing: vanity

October 23, 1905

McRae failed to sell the St. Louis paper to Nathan Frank. In a way Scripps was glad, telling Bob Paine:

"McRae has a failing. It is vanity . . . . In St. Louis, I have let him have his way . . . . McRae is an old dog to learn new tricks, and he has got either to prove McRaeism a success or forever hold his peace . . . . [If the *Star-Chronicle* were sold] I would be glad to get the money into the treasury, but . . . . it would be a year before we could transact any business in McRae's presence because he would insist on taking up all our time by bragging about his feat."

Confused by dust and smoke

November 21, 1905

McRae fell ill, but EWS refused to let up, saying he must make or break it in St. Louis. To his lawyer J.C. Harper:

"I sit out here at Miramar, a great way off from all the business I control. I am on a hill, as it were, looking down on a field of battle . . . . I have long years of experience and a retentive memory . . . . I am not a great general, perhaps in nature, but . . .

my way of doing business . . . [has given] me the experience of a general . . . . You . . . and the other boys are . . . in your own cloud of dust and smoke. Were any of you where I am, you would certainly see thing very differently . . . .

"I will neither drive McRae out of the concern, nor permit him to leave it, if he will consent to stay and do his plain duty to it . . . .

"However, it is more likely as time goes on and events happen you will join Paine in urging me to be lenient and merciful. There will be just as much wisdom in your doing this as there would be by an onlooker of a surgical operation for a case of cancer, who would beg the surgeon to cut out only a part of the cancer to save the patient immediate pain—urge him in fact to leave the disease in the body, in such a condition to require more operations that would otherwise be unnecessary, and hence far more pain in the long run."

". . . fish or cut bait"

December 26, 1905

To lawyer Harper:
". . . Mac now stands as one of my antagonists, devoting almost whole energy to his personal interests . . . . There will be only one head of the concern . . . . And I am going to be the head. If Mac will not consent . . . and sets up a claim of duality, I will set him aside . . . . In other words, Mac has got to fish or cut bait. He has got to be with me, or against me . . . ."

Mistress and maid

After meeting with MacRae at Miramar, EWS wrote to L.T. Atwood:

"McRae learned from me exactly where he was at, and exactly what I would do . . . . I was not only frank in my talk with him, but refrained from no statement, no adjectives, no epithets—harsh, disagreeable, or friendly—that would serve to impress upon his mind all my ideas . . . .

"My relations with Mac must continue personal, intimate, and confidential, but that condition must not imply a position of equality between us . . . . Our true relationship is more similar . . . to that existing between the mistress of the house and the maid of all work."

Can't do all the thinking

Finally EWS had to admit he no longer could stay on top of everything happening. He wrote Mac:

"This concern is too big for me to do all the thinking. The cabinet and its various members have got to do a lot of it . . . . I am not anxious to take up any subject which does not absolutely require my personal attention."

Meddling

November 15, 1905

Scripps angrily accuses his partner of again meddling in Cincinnati editorial affairs, writing him:

"You do not see the difference between making money in order to run good newspapers, and running good newspapers to make money."

". . . my guardian"

December 6, 1906

Finally deciding to fire McRae, EWS confidentially so told his successor, L.T. Atwood:

"It took me a long time to realize, but I finally did, that Mr. McRae considers himself to really be my guardian and me a rather brilliant, erratic, changeable person whom he has . . . not allowed to injure himself and yet to be allowed to feel he was . . . having his own way and doing things."

Humbling Mac's ego

April 13, 1907

To J.C. Harper, EWS almost gloats over ousting his partner, asserting he resented Mac's "looking out for Number One," and considering himself rival to EWS:

"I struck him in his most vital part, the humbling of his egotism . . . . Mr. McRae for some time has been almost valueless to the concern."

"I am the concern"

September 18, 1907

Still taking a hard line on his old partner, EWS tells Bob Paine:

"Mac decided I was a hypocrite for business purposes . . . that he was the great man and I was a hanger-on. I am the concern. If I am false or unjust, the concern has these faults and is not fit to live."

Jim lays down the law

EWS has installed young son Jim as "king" of the concern, and praises him to McRae:

"Though I abdicated, I was prone to resent my loss of authority. It is significant that this young fellow should, so soon after his induction, begin laying down the law for the concern, not only to you but to me . . . .

"Jim handles thousands of dollars as freely as I ever handled hundreds, and sometimes this makes me wince a little."

AN ADLESS NEWSPAPER

"The common vulgar friend"

August 10, 1910

For years EWS wanted to publish a newspaper that carried no advertising. He always feared merchants—he called them "counter-jumpers"—might try to control his policies by the weight of their advertising dollars. He tried to hold down advertising content, limiting his *San Francisco News*, for instance, to three columns of ads a day. He thought his papers could survive only on the one-cent sales price. Finally he teamed up with Negley Cochran, his Toledo editor, to start the adless paper in Chicago.

It did not start quickly, but EWS had a clear idea of what he wanted, writing Cochran:

"You and I were gloating over the prospect of having such freedom from commercialism as would permit us to publish whatever we wanted to without regard to the enmity or favor of certain classes.

"We were thinking of the editorials we could print which would be of benefit to the masses. In fact, we had our heads up so high they were bumping the stars.

"Now there is another freedom I want . . . to be absolutely indifferent to the contempt of all classes . . . . I want the newspaper to be the common vulgar friend and companion of the common vulgar crowd, of which if I am not a member, I would like to be.

"We do not propose to have any ideals that are higher than those of our friends—our patron readers. The great masses of the people have ideals that are thoroughly respectable, and I do not propose to educate them to higher levels of thought, than such as could be reasonably expected of men and women who have to labor their lives through for, at best, a little more than a competence, and savings for rainy days and old age.

"I do want to inform them correctly and truthfully on all these matters in which they are interested and only on such matters as they, despite their toil and lack of culture and leisure, could be interested in. I want to establish a press that will be an aid to the people in organizing themselves for their own advantage, and such little advancement of their interests as are practicable in this day and age.

"Such a paper would not give us much space for preachments and lectures. The moral tone must be of such a character as to be considered very low indeed as compared with the ideals possessed by the great majority with whom we have had social contact nearly all our lives.

"There is a class of literature in the old yellow-backed dime novels, and in such a paper as the *Police Gazette* once was, which might come nearer to what I am thinking of than anything that is to be found in the average journal of the most democratic proclivities, daily, weekly, or monthly, now published.

"In the religious field, the Salvation Army is occupying a position somewhat similar to what we could strive for in our new journalism.

"In fact, Cochran, it would be difficult to find amongst journalists of any class, men who have not been trained into what would be called snobs by our readers.

"Perhaps you and I might organize, capitalize and direct such a newspaper as we are thinking of, but only a small amount of matter that we publish should appear in the literary form we are accustomed to. We never lived the dollar-a-day life long enough to acquire the dollar-a-day material and spiritual level."

Needs reckless daring

September 28, 1910

Cochran, sidetracked by involvement in Ohio politics, got this prod from the boss:

"I fully appreciate the peculiarity of this venture. I can understand how you might be greatly attracted to the idea, only after a time to waken to a more practical and sane view . . . .

"If you ever feel the least shiver of doubt, I want to know it . . . . There are going to be oceans of struggle . . . and success or failure will depend entirely upon the hardihood if not the reckless daring of the adventurers.

An oddball infant

September 28, 1911

On this day, EWS's adless brainchild was born. Called the *Chicago Day Book*, it was oddball in several ways. Not really a newspaper, more of a book—32 pages each 6 by 10 inches, two columns to a page, small headlines. EWS didn't like the name, but admitted, "Of course if the flower is sweet and pretty it does not matter whether it is called a rose or something else."

Cochran didn't have his act together. The odd-ball paper jiggled and jagged. Scripps was on him like a duck on a Junebug. The *Day Book* cost $100 a day to publish, and could break even with 30,000 circulation. In the first month sales were only 100 copies a day—one dollar!

Ninety-cent dollars

November 15, 1911

Scripps tried to sympathize, but also scolded. He wrote Cochran:

"I fully recognize the apparent absurdity of shooting birds with a cannon . . ." [Later] "Any fool can do a large business by selling dollars for 90 cents."

Shut down?

December 15, 1911

An angry telegram to Cochran:

"Your plans are all wrong. Even if they were all right I would shut down sooner than go on with them. Get a [circulation] man who believes in my method and give it a try. Don't talk about this even in the office."

To Cochran:
"You have been just beating the devil around the bush . . . . I only wanted the paper to make its way with the people, slowly (if that were necessary), but solely by means of its interesting character to the reader.

"Why can't you try *MY* plan? You will have to try it sooner or later; or else before I shut the paper down, I will get somebody else to try it . . . . I am waiting impatiently for you to get down to business . . . . I am ready to bet a thousand dollars to one you haven't adopted my idea, and don't know what it is."

All scold

To Cochran:
"Tonight I have looked over a number of *Day Books*. They are full of appeals to working men's minds—to their sense of justice or injustice. There are to be found no things that will cause a man to forget that he has to work—that he suffers.

"There is nothing to make him laugh for the pure joy of being able to laugh, or to appeal to the commonplace interests. It is all uplift, argument and scold, and no fun or frolic and no common everyday plain workingman's gossip and 'chow rag'."

Scripps offered his own formula for giving "readers a comfortable, interesting half-hour's occupation reading your sheet.

"What we want in at least 31 out of 32 pages is the kind of thing that any human being, whether in the professor's chair, the salon of the merchant prince, behind the counter, in the blacksmith's shop, in the kitchen, on the streetcar platform, or on the curb would be interested in, that is to say, would thoroughly enjoy. The 32nd page is enough to furnish all the uplift and intellectual pablum that our duty could possibly call for.

"Try giving your readers something in your 31 pages that won't cause them to think, that won't even invite them to think. Let them spend the time they devote to reading these pages in entire forgetfulness of rights and wrongs, of ambitions and disappointments. Laughable trivialities that can catch and hold the eye, and lead it on from paragraph to paragraph, are good enough stuff.

"You see, Cochran, the world of journalism, unlike that of fiction, is today almost wholly composed of matter that makes men and women think, or think they think, or think they ought to think. That task of public enlightenment is so thoroughly and all-pervasively presented that our labors in this field are not necessities cried for by the people.

"Let us amuse our folks first. Let us gather around us a great audience first and then we can slip over into their minds unsuspected by them some bit of information, some pegs on which thoughts will hang, some things that will help them to help themselves and their country.

"Let us quit teaching and lecturing and instructing as the main part of our business, or as any more than one-thirty-second part of our occupation, and devote the rest of ourselves to being just common, plain, everyday, interesting good-natured, laugh-provoking fellows.

"Just what kind of stuff would I advise you to put in your paper—jokes that will make very common people and especially young boys and girls laugh—love stories that are pleasant, that have something of a thrill of sentiment that any woman can feel, and if possible, love stories that will make even a hard-working, tired old working-man father grin as he reads it of an evening—cook receipts [recipes]—and perhaps some information as to how a poor girl can renovate a hat ribbon, or a poor boy can cheaply clean up last year's hat to make it look decent this year—how to clean an old pipe or mend a piece of furniture.

"(Parenthetically, I will remark I believe the most acceptable items that can appear in a newspaper—most readers of all newspapers are poor people—are those which will instruct a man or woman, boy or girl, how to make a public show of apparent prosperity on the smallest conceivable income.)

"The intellectual tone of the *Day Book* is at least 75 per cent too high. The manager should associate with no one making more than $15 a week, or read any literature higher than a farmer's weekly or a dime novel.

"He should soak himself in the atmosphere of the proletariat for a few months. I don't want him to study and think about them. I want him to feel them."

An honest salesman?

Cochran was flabbergasted to find some canvassers were turning in false circulation "starts." Scripps wasn't fazed:

"Any fellow who will do this, if properly trained with a club, will get results . . . . Unfortunately, there are few men who have the double qualifications—that of being perfectly honest and that of being a good salesman.

"There are some honest men who are good salesman perhaps, but few good salesmen that are overburdened with honesty."

Flabby heart's pride

April 28, 1913

Finally Scripps detected a spark—when Cochran published some down-to-earth "Personal Notes." EWS let out a whoop:

"Neg, this flabby old heart of mine just swelled and swelled with pride. I even felt a suspicion of moisture in my eyes. To be the father of such a publication, I feel to be the greatest honor that I have experienced.

"If the *Day Book* can stay on this course it will make it impossible for Chicago journalism to re-

main the disgraceful thing that it has been . . . .
The Scripps papers, I am proud to claim, have
developed into a tremendous, but largely unrecog-
nized influence in the United States. Neg, do not let
the *Day Book* fail!"

"Supreme vulgarity"

Unfortunately, Cochran slipped out of sync
again, went too high-brow, totally unable "to wal-
low in friendly intercourse with the mire of humanity." EWS wondered what Clarence Darrow, who
had journalistic ambitions, could do with the *Day
Book*. He also wondered if Cochran "knew too
much, was perhaps too honest," in a letter to Byron
Canfield, his chief West Coast editor:

"The only thing needed in the *Day Book* is
supreme vulgarity. The great majority of men especially in a city like Chicago can be happy—at least
for brief periods of time—although their clothes
and their houses are full of vermin; although their
bellies are full of coarse unpalatable food; although
they are surrounded with filth and stench; although
their wives and daughters lack virtue, and their
sons and fathers commit brutal crimes . . . .

"How can a clean-minded, clean-housed, clean-
clothed, clean-fed man speak or write language that
can be understood and give expression to the feelings that are not only common but almost universal
among the sordid, sodden, poverty-possessed?"

A big work

Finally the *Day Book* showed promise of breaking even. Scripps boasted to Lincoln Steffens:

". . . It should be comparatively easy for other men, younger and hence more vigorous, to establish other such papers . . . . I should feel then that despite all my shortcomings I shall have done a big man's big life work, when, if ever I shall have demonstrated that the people can have a free press, not only without having it subsidized or endowed, but a free press that will not only support but magnificently reward those who conduct its various units."

The death knell

March 12, 1917

With America heading into World War I, EWS decided to stop the *Day Book* experiment. He blamed defeat on Cochran being too high-brow, but accepted a share of blame. He refused to surrender on the concept, saying in a letter instructing Jim to settle on a date to fold the paper:

"The adless theory is practicable; I expect to someday successfully develop it . . . . The editor makes the newspaper . . . . Scripps was too old and didn't much care a damn for anything and didn't have to succeed . . . . But Neg had had his fill of glory, had become . . . rich. He was older. He quit thinking, and was only remembering. He had more time to drink, and he liked to drink. He became sort of a gentleman-farmer. Age and conditions robbed both Neg and Scripps of all their virilities.

"One cannot build a big, successful property as a fair or amusement."

[Six years old, lacking two months, the little oddball paper was killed on July 6, 1917.]

Julia Anne Scripps, sister and
confidant.

Julia A. Osborne Scripps, mother.

Ellen Browning Scripps, sister and
lifelong mentor.

James E. Scripps, brother.

I/EWS

Ellen Browning Scripps in later life.

Circa 1844.

On his yacht "Ohio." Early 20's.

Postcard of the Scripps yacht Ohio, at Algiers.

Office at Miramar.

EWS, left, when city editor at the Detroit Evening News, with brother George H. Scripps, center, and Robert Ross. Circa 1875.

Miramar ranch house, designed by E.W. after the Empress Carlotta's castle, Trieste.

Courtyard at Miramar with fountain from the St. Louis Exposition.

Wife Nackie with daughters Dolla, left, and Nackey, veranda at Miramar. Circa 1898.

With his sons, left to right, John, Jim and Bob at Miramar. Circa 1898.

Detroit Evening News building. Circa 1890.

X/EWS

Milton A. McRae, partner and business associate. Circa 1912.

Roy W. Howard, left, with Joseph C. Grew, U.S. Ambassador to Japan, after an audience with Emperor Hirohito in 1933.

ROY W. HOWARD

". . . only bright and clever"

June 5, 1908

John Vandercook, president of United Press, died suddenly. Roy W. Howard, who had been Van's own back-up choice, boldly asked for the job. EWS, to his own son Jim and others:

"That fellow Howard is perhaps the most desirable candidate . . . His extreme youth [Roy was then 25], the fact that we caught him so soon, and that he feels himself naturally a press association man . . . are all very strong arguments in his favor. He may be only bright and clever. A few months or a year longer of service will let us know more about him."

"Fight your way upward"

October 7, 1908

Howard persisted, writing he was "not afraid" and willing to keep "plugging and grinding." EWS still hesitated, replying:

"You are a young man, which is no crime . . . . You will have a considerable career in our concern . . . . If you don't get one chance, you'll get others . . . . My personal advice is: continue as you have begun; fight your way upward, and win by convincing others of your merit, and refuse, even when opportunity affords itself, to gain anything by personal favor."

Youth hurts Roy

November 5, 1908

EWS declined to invite RWH to Miramar editorial conference, telling "Ham" Clark:

"Howard should, and must if he is going to succeed, fight his way up rather than be hoisted into position. Not the least part of my bias toward Howard is based on this fact of extreme, comparative youthfulness . . .

"If Howard had twice his present vigor it would be better for all concerned."

"If Clark is rattled . . ."

March 25, 1909

Howard got a lucky break. UP boss "Ham" Clark cracked up. EWS didn't want to bring in an outsider. He wrote Jim:

"That young boy, Howard, is very young, but that is nothing against him. He has a frail constitution; that is the one blemish. But if Clark is rattled, then as between Clark and Howard, there can be no question about the latter being the best man."

Pore-oozing confidence

In a disquisition written in 1917, EWS recalls his first meeting with RWH, at Miramar about 1908:

"He was a striking individual, very small in stature, a large head and eyes that appeared to be windows for a rather unusual intellect.

"His manner was forceful and the reverse of modest. Gall was . . . in every tone and every word he voiced. There was ambition, self-respect, and forcefulness oozing out of every pore . . .

"Since those days Howard has learned to affect some degree of deference . . . in my presence; but in my first interview with him, he did not reveal, and I do not believe he experienced, the least feeling of awe . . . . He was so completely and exhuberantly frank that it was impossible for me to feel any resentment . . ."

EWS recalls, a few years later, how surprised "and tickled" he was with himself when he gave way to his propensity for experimentation to put Roy in charge of the wire service. The result? "Howard made good . . . Howard continued to make good, and as he made good, the United Press made good and began to grow into a property that had actual value."

Expects bosses to fuss

May 25, 1922

When he eventually teamed up son Bob, 26, and RWH, 39, EWS observed in his diary he expected a certain amount of squabbling between them:

"I was convinced that there would often be contention between them, and that it was really desirable that they should not be in constant accord and agreement.

"If they both felt alike and thought alike and worked alike, then it would only be a waste of time and money to employ two men to do what one could do."

". . . smoke-screen for Bob"

July 19, 1922

McRae had bested EWS in getting custody of their joint grandson, John Paul. EWS wrote to Ellen:

"I am old and disillusioned, to such an extent that McRae's attitude has not surprised me at all . . . . [He] is just a two-legged human being, just the same kind of ordinary animal that I am myself.

"I decided . . . to gradually change the name of our concern from Scripps-McRae to Scripps-Howard. Howard is just another smoke-screen that

McRae has always been to me. It has always been a matter of my convenience and comfort that everybody should run to McRae instead of me and McRae knew a hundred prominent citizens over the country to every one I knew.

"Now I think Howard has something of the same instinct for the limelight as McRae has and I think he will be just as good a smoke-screen for Bob as McRae has been for me, if Bob wants a smoke-screen as I have always wanted one."

Drive . . . lead . . . produce

November 29, 1922

Even three weeks after Scripps-Howard was formed, RWH was badgering EWS for detailed instructions. Scripps informed Ellen:

"I had not more than five minutes with him personally. I told him it was his business to do what he should do . . . could do . . . By sheer force of character and ability, to persuade—to drive—to lead—and produce results. [Scripps did not intend to grant what Howard wanted: full authority.]

"My own scheme of doing things has always been to hold in my own hands full authority, and to place in other hands all the responsibility."

Why profits shared

When RWH and Bob tried to withdraw part of their stock bonus in cash, EWS wrote a diary note that every dime must be reinvested in the business:

"My intention was not to be generous in my treatment of the two men but generous in my treatment of the concern. I have been perfectly frank, expecially in my talk with Howard, in explaining the object I had in mind in sharing with him my increased profits.

"I said to him, 'The more stock you get the more certain am I of your having a continuing interest in, and being compelled by that interest, to devote a large part of your attention to the concern . . .' "

On going it alone

July 24, 1924

RWH threatened a time or two to jump ship. EWS called his bluff when he talked about striking out on his own, writing Ellen:

"Howard asked bluntly whether I didn't think he could do better for himself if he left the concern. To this I answered that he had for so long a time been living a symbiotic life—depending upon and being depended upon—that I thought it would be impossible for him to stand alone.

"Then Howard said he was rich enough at the time of *The Pittsburgh Press* purchase that he could have bought it for himself instead of the concern. My reply was that I put him in just such a position as to enable him to do such a thing because of my high respect for his ability which of course included his intelligence and his morality.

"I wouldn't predict that Roy would make a failure if he were to go into business on his own account. He is an extremely able man and has proved it during the past years when he has been with me."

PULITZER & HEARST

". . . Pulitzer is wild"

August 23, 1894

To Ellen:

"The *St. Louis Post-Dispatch* is thoroughly rattled. Pulitzer is wild at discovery of having been so distanced without being warned. he is discharging his men right and left.

"McRae, Young and Osborn [EWS's men in charge of the *Chronicle*] have been each offered good salary and stock, and turned him down.

"Pulitzer is preparing to give us a battle royal in his effort to regain the prestige of his paper."

Fiasco in Chicago

Spring, 1900

With EWS backing, Bob Paine impetuously launched a penny paper, the *Chicago Press,* April 11, 1900. He bit off too much for a one-man show and went haywire. Scripps sent in another editor, and at first considered the paper a promising. "child of my brain." Yet he seemed to think his ownership was a secret, writing Ellen:

"Do not talk to anyone about the *Chicago Press.* I am commonly considered insane by my friends, a fool by my employees, and a rascal by all others."

Enter Hearst

Hearst decided to invade Chicago with the *American* to be launched July, 4, 1900, with 225,000-copies-an-hour presses. To Ellen:

"Hearst's plant cost a cool $250,000. He has one thousand men in his office, four or five of his top generals here. My hopes? Oh, I don't know. We will be up against show, splurge and bigness. He will fight the *Journal* [owned by brother James] . . . . cripple and embarrass James . . . . It will be five years before Hearst even learns the *Chicago Press* exists."

Risking $100 a day

July 18, 1900

McRae, frightened, wanted to close down the little *Chicago Press,* but the boss resisted, writing his partner:

"I concede Hearst is filling every crack and cranny of my proposed field in Chicago—except one. It is barely possible that the merit of being little, light-weight, easily carried, and quickly read will be a sufficient foundation on which to build a paper capable of competing with such a people's paper as Hearst appears to be making. It is worth one hundred dollars a day for a short time to continue the experiment. . . ."

Very short. On July 28, 1900—a Saturday when by-the-week union employment obligations were fulfilled—EWS quietly folded the infant paper.

Hearst for President

January 24, 1908

Curiously, Scripps felt the only man on the 1908 political scene "big enough to do the job" as President was William Randolph Hearst, writing Bob Paine:

"He certainly is a man of giant proportions . . . [Hearst has] that one great quality of all great heroes who have been able to move the world: a supreme egotism.

". . . This country has got to fight . . . with men and ships . . . . Hearst knows this . . . and will face the facts . . . . When we do fight, Hearst and Roosevelt are the only ones who would do things themselves. With a Taft, a Bryan or even a Hughes in the White House, the nation would have to do its own thinking as well as its own fighting."

"Hearst . . . following me"

May 4, 1924

After EWS started the Baltimore *Post,* Hearst invaded the city, too, prompting this letter to Ellen:

"Hearst seems to be following me up pretty regularly, although he spends millions where I spend hundreds of thousands, and he borrows money by the million where so far I have had no occasion to borrow anything although I estimate that (including the purchase price of the Youngstown paper, the Indianapolis paper, and the Pittsburgh paper and some other things), our unpaid obligations amount to seven and one-half million dollars . . . . The big figures . . . sometimes startle me and sometimes scare me.

"I was never quite bold enough to prophesy the failure of William R. Hearst. The farthest I ever went was to say that according to all my own principles and ideas, Hearst ought to be a failure. Instead he has been more successful than I have been."

Hearst's rising star

September 4, 1925

Looking back in a disquisition titled, *"New York—1876—1925—and Me":*

"At this date William Randolph Hearst is recognized as the greatest of American newspapermen. I own more newspapers than Hearst, but Hearst owns bigger newspaper than mine. I really do not know what Hearst is worth in way of money, and to be perfectly frank, I do not know what I am worth. I only feel pretty sure that Hearst controls newspaper property valued at two or three times the value I put on my newspaper holdings.

"But Hearst's star actually rose after I had retired from business, or thought I had retired, some 35 years ago . . . . All the old great journalists of New York have disappeared . . . . I consider myself a glittering example of what may happen to a man if he succeeds in living long enough . . . ."

COURAGE

Carrying a pistol

Winter, 1878

From the earliest days of *The Cleveland Press,*
Scripps began carrying a revolver in his hip "pistol" pocket, explaining in his autobiography:
"I knew I would kill somebody if I was touched
. . . . During the first 10 years of my career as a
journalist it was not uncommon for editors to be
shot, or for editors to shoot other people. Horse-
whipping of editors was sometimes indulged in, and
more often threatened."

Needing a six-shooter

1915

His autobiography also relates:
"When a man is fully prepared to take any risk
. . . or pay any penalty in order to accomplish some
one thing, it rarely ever occurs that a man has to
take any risk or pay any penalty.
"I heard an old Texan once say that in his
country a man who had a pistol seldom had to use
it, but when he did not happen to have a gun
around, he was sure to need it mighty bad."

". . . reckless onslaught"

To Ellen:
"All my victories have been won by reckless onslaught. A charge is always better than a siege. By vehement self-confidence and egotism and arrogance, if you will, I have won more in days than patient merit would have gained in years."

Fires his cousin

October 8, 1897

After moving his cousin Willis Osborn from Cleveland to St. Louis to manage the *Chronicle,* EWS found Osborn dickering with Pulitzer for a job (which he later took). Scripps had Osborn discharged, but didn't duck his role in the affair, writing his cousin:

"I am not coward enough to let you believe that any but I am responsible for the blow. Others may have wished the down-throw and none could have accomplished it as long as I felt your employment was not a detriment to the concern . . . .

"I must as a necessity open my heart and mind to men who hold such positions as yours. When you told me . . . that you had a right to use such confidence for the benefit of a competitor who

would pay your price, my mouth was closed . . . .
After that I could tell you none of my plans . . . ."

"A gun . . . and an ugly look"

Men on his *Los Angeles Record* were arrested
at a poker game and accused the police of a vendet-
ta. Writing the business manager, EWS advised
using "some adroitness" to get out of "a very delicate position" which could be misconstrued as a
"personal quarrel":

"Don't seek sympathy . . . but stand up and
fight your own battles for the public interest . . . .

"In several instances my associates were at-
tacked and had to fight for it. There is great
difference between courage and daredeviltry. Seldom is there any necessity for exposure to real
danger. Keep out of crowds. Keep away from fra-
cases. Never permit yourself to be in places where
any excuse can be made for police or bullies to your
own detriment. Don't walk the streets at night. Go
in couples.

"I have on a number of occasions been threatened with horse-whippings, thrashings, knifings,
and shootings. I was not really very brave. I used to
feel uneasy . . . was really timid. I took care of
myself. I never took back water in my paper. I
never abandoned a fight through fear.

"And I am nearly 50 years old without ever
having been struck at, or having a vile epithet
applied to me in person. I acknowledge that on two
or three occasions I was saved from such affronts

from the fact that I had a gun . . . that I was big in person, had an ugly look . . . the reputation of always being ready . . . and supposed to shoot straight.

"Finally, I would advise you to keep your eyes always open, be always on the alert for treachery, and keep your nerve."

HOW TO SUCCEED

"Claptrap humbug . . . ?"

March 29, 1881

To Annie:
"Am I claptrap humbug, or a genius? I have not
made up my mind. I rather suspect the former. If
that be so, I have done well. If the latter, there are
other avenues for quick flying ambition, if I do not
choose the slower and surer path that now lies
before me."

"Money doesn't make money"

December, 1878

After James E. Scripps clamped an expense
down-hold on EWS and John Sweeney at the fledg-
ling *Penny Press,* EWS perceived a valuable lesson:
"There, in that case, was demonstrated to me
. . .that men make money and money doesn't make
money. It is the man that makes the newspaper, not
the man's capital."

Pluck

October 21, 1883

To Annie:

"It requires a great deal of good sense to keep a fortune, but to make money—bah! Any baby who has got pluck and knows how to manage can do that."

". . . I've got to win"

November 12, 1883

To Annie:

"I am engaged in another of those desperate conspiracies against my fate and fortune . . . I have bought controlling stock of the *Chronicle,* and in one fell swoop have plunged into a personal dept of $40,000! Of course I intend to make $100,000, at least, but what if I don't! I have shut my eyes and jumped in and am already getting accustomed to my new situation.

"This dirty town beat me once. Wonder if it is fated that the grave of all my hopes is to be filled with St. Louis mud? Oh well! What difference will it make?

"I will soon cease to think about the possibility of defeat and shall be fighting here with such a fight as you would not think your lazy brother capable of even in defense of his own life . . . . I am studying . . . for the coming battle. It is not the nicest kind of work. I prefer to charge the enemy rather than build earthworks and lay plans . . . . I expect to win, of course . . . . Why, I am playing a game of whist where every card lost represents a $1,000 bill. I've got to win, or lose big money!"

"I am turned skinflint"

June 18, 1884

In debt to his brothers for $48,000 and paying interest of $60 a week, EWS—on his 30th birth-day—writes Annie:

"Work has already begun showing the world I was born a Scripps and hence am a close-fisted financier. I must take a firm, unpitying stand in looking out for Number One. Sick employees must be docked for time lost. Poor men must work at the lowest market price. Widows and orphans must seek elsewhere a philanthropist. Hard-ups borrow elsewhere. I am turned skinflint."

Hard times in St. Louis

September 12, 1884

Up against it in St. Louis, EWS explains to

Ellen about having to fire loyal staffers and cut salaries:

"I go to the office at 7 a.m. I sit down and work all day. I eat three meals in 24 hours, get tired, get mad and swear often . . . go home and sleep well . . . . James [brother] says he rejoices in my dilemma because I am being taught by experience a lesson that will insure my future success.

"Well, I am fighting it and so until the first of the year I will have to get down to 'one bean a day' when, if I am lucky, the old horse will die."

Frederick the Great

EWS reads Thomas Carlyle's *Frederick the Great* and is struck by marked similarities between his life and that of the hot-headed combative Prussian king, writing Ellen:

"I have been trying to extract from this book some lessons myself. You will have to laugh when I tell you what lesson I think I have taken to heart, and I think I did not need a Carlyle or a Frederick the Great to teach it to me.

"It is to stick to my own opinions and by force or strategy if possible maintain them, but failing that, by sheer endurance wear out all opposition."

"Wild steam engine"

EW develops his "league" idea and opens a New York bureau for cheaper telegraph news to Scripps Publishing Co. papers in Cleveland, Detroit, St. Louis and Cincinnati, telling Annie:

"I feel that the wild steam engine of my youth is finally hitched to a giant force for good or evil . . . . Where before I thought of business as a pastime, an employment, an amusement, an exhilarating exercise of the faculties, it has now become purely and simply a great duty . . . to family, offspring, a thousand others, employees and friends . . . dependents for my judgment whether they live well or ill. . . .

"Whole millions whose lives depend on how well I do my work. I am no longer a boy. It is not time to waste in dreaming or rest, but a time for work— work with my own hands and brain."

"A captain man"

After gaining the leadership of the four-paper league, EWS writes Ellen:

"Now is my crucial test. Flunkeyism, flattery and all do their utmost to make a fool of me, and if they do not succeed I will indeed have cause for pride. My real anxiety is to find out just what my stuff is. I have always been a student and a thinker and a self-styled philosopher. My anxiety is to find out whether I am not also a captain man with a general's uniform on."

"What I think best"

February 8, 1889

When brother George challenged his authority in running the *Detroit News,* EWS reports to Ellen:

"As I do not care for either glory or riches and all the interest I have in this business is to see it grow into something worth admiring, I can without any credit or self-sacrifice go on doing what I think best, resigned and feeling happy if I lose.

"If I had no wife or only an ugly wife, or if I had no children or only a parcel of nasty brats, if I were anxious for wealth, if I loved the flattery of a world of little men, all might be different and then I do not think [brothers] James or George would long be able to curb me if they wanted to, and I would think twice of myself to once of the business."

"I've got enough"

EWS takes personal charge of *The Cincinnati Post* because "Cincinnati is the gateway between the north and south and its journals should be the leaders in the movement of peace and better treatment and goodwill between the two sections." He writes Ellen:

"I am determined to make a good new paper . . . I could have made $100,000 a year in the next three years but what's the good if by so doing I must run my papers on the business principles that govern a brewery, a soap factory, or an ordinary clothing store.

"I've got enough—too much. We all have too much. I would be damned if I make no better use of my talent than to leave no proof of my success after I'm dead than a pile of money and an example that money-making was my chief object of existence."

The Lycurgus Code

To Ellen:

"Remember the story of the old Greek Lycurgus, who giving his people a code of laws, made them mean to keep them until his return and then went off never returning.

"Something on the same principle I have given my men tasks hard to perform, hastening away before circumstances may occur which may cause me to consent to less performance, leaving them bound by honor and self-pride to meet me on my return with accomplished results and no excuses.

"I have all my life had my own plan of administration. It has several features. It proscribes doing anything that another can do . . . . It is to develop men rather than imposing on them responsibilities and by a twice-long and intricate course of instruction . . . . Its aim is to limit the scope of action to a chief to a constantly descreasing set of subjects, each piece of detail being turned over to some other who has developed a capacity for it.

"Each year the chief should become less important to the maintenance of what he has established with more liberty and greater capacity to enlarge the business . . . . In 20 years I have done not more than 10 essential things and 20 other important things.

"I might have done more of both had I not wasted so much time and effort on doing things that I could have let others do, thus depriving myself of time and energy to think more and act harder."

No gratis stock

February 16, 1897

George Shives got the idea EWS was presenting

him some gratis stock in the *Kansas City World* for his editorial direction of the wobbly newspaper but was quickly straightened out:

"I dare not advise a man where to invest his money. The *World* future depends on its management, lots of hard work, and risks to run. I never made a dollar except under the most disagreeable conditions and never expect to. I never found a treasure. I never inherited, and am glad that my own intellectual strength has never been atrophied by such hard luck . . . .

"I am one of those independent, vain, and cranky men who refuse to accept favors . . . where you have all to gain and nothing to lose."

The AP challenge

May 23, 1897

EWS rejects "insulting" offer to join the Associated Press, and launches rival wire service, Scripps-McRae Telegrams. From Chicago, he wrote Nackie:

"It is this SMT business that is going to detain me and exact my attention. I would certainly like to have you with me but I have got to keep a clear head and attend to business . . . . The work I will have to do will also be too arduous to permit of my not having the intervals between my hours of labor for complete rest and relaxation. I cannot leave the hard labor of business to devote the rest of my time to explaining that I am too busy and too much bothered to even think whether my actions may not be misunderstood.

"There would be only this advantage of your

being with me in these times: You would learn the utter fallacy of your belief that I, a trained and expert business man, could live within reach of business without being wholly absorbed by it.

"You would see me consuming under the pressure of business more stimulants even under other trying conditions. . . .

"I can confidently assert that I have in the two weeks since I left Miramar spent or obligated myself to expend more money than I have spent in six years in California and that these investments are not so wise, all things considered, as those others. I have deliberately chosen to spend $30,000 a year in this one enterprise sooner then submit to the least abridgement of my personal independence. *Now,* that being done, I have got to see to making the money to pay for it. Never doubt that I'll do it." [Later he rechristened SMT, making it SMPA, the Scripps-McRae Press Association, before moving to the name United Press in 1907.]

Razzle-dazzle Will

Summer, 1901

Like a moth to flame, EWS was attracted to newspapermen with the roguish glint of bravado. One was Will Kellogg, married to brother Will's daughter. EW wrote his lawyer, J.C. Harper:

"I admit that Kellogg can razzle-dazzle me as no other man can. One day I feel he is 'bust' and the next day I feel he is worth a million . . . . Sometime when you find me too cocksure about things remind me. It may make me swear, but it will do me good."

"Control everything"

April 21, 1902

To Ellen:

"I never have been and do not believe that I am in position where any one man or any dozen men, is absolutely essential for the successful prosecution of my plans. There has never been a time when I have not considered it very likely that I might have to dispense with the services of the most important of my staff, and I have steadily pursued such a course of selection and training of men as to make anything possible.

"I do not say that any change would not be very costly. I can only say that no change would be made that would be disastrous. There is only one situation that I would consider fatal, and that would be to find myself with my hands bound so that I could not, at my will, control everything that depends upon me, and that I depend on . . . .

"I have a lot of knotty problems to be solved, as you see—a lot of hard work cut out for me, and I have more; a lot of conditions that have pretty thoroughly taxed all my powers and resolutions. I do not expect to come out with flying colors, but I shall go home with almost every plan and every situation well worked out in advance, so that the strain that will fall upon me when I get there will not be that of thinking.

"It will only be the result of having to do those things which I have already made up my mind to do.

"This is an entirely confidential letter . . . . Please take good care of it."

FAME & EDUCATION

"Educating myself"

May 12, 1883

From Paris, ready to go home, Scripps writes Annie:

"What I have preferred is to devote all my time to educating myself. I have not a mind for the minutia. I am more given to generalities. I am still too young to have a strong grasp, but I can better handle the whole effect than the partial . . . .

"I am to a certain extent a ruminator. I have swallowed many a chunk of unmasticated facts which years hence I must recall and ruminate."

Dangers of praise

June 10, 1886

James E. Scripps in a magazine article listed McRae as one of America's "twenty greatest" newspapermen, slighting EWS, and McRae wrote that he felt this made Scripps a little jealous. EWS snapped back:

"I resent as an insult to myself those sycophantic or insincere offerings . . . . Never in my life have I felt any covetousness of your fame—any desire that I should have said of me what has been said of you . . . . The Scripps-McRae League is neither you, nor me, nor us two and George. It is every man in it . . . .

"You have not yet shaken off the consciousness of being a hired man . . . . Drink your fill of the sweets of praise *now* so that you will have become surfeited of the stuff, before the taste of it will become dangerous to all of us."

Tutor at Miramar

May 1, 1898

To McRae:

"My idea of education is signified by the original Latin of which it is a derivation—which indicates a drawing out—that means the development of what is original. My quarrel with the school and college is that both more or less suppress what is original, attempt to build up what does not exist in the child's mind and in fact by training attempt to produce a mind and a character similar to that of the teacher or professor.

"That would suit anyone intending to be a teacher, but it seems to me that it would be very injurious to the child who is expected to have any other career.

"Most businessmen are so engrossed in the business of piling up millions for our children that we give them really very little attention . . . . We hire nurses, governesses, tutors, and buy college advantage on the one side, and on the other are only too glad to shirk our duty of personal attention . . . ."

MIRAMAR

A view from Eden

June 16, 1893

EWS had to rush to Miramar in the summer of 1893 because his mother was dying, and wrote Nackie:

"I am sitting up in my office room. I have the east windows closed and all the south and west openings admitting the sea breeze. I can see far off to the southwest La Jolla and westward the sea; all in this . . . summer haze that I have described to you. It is claimed to be an intensely hot day . . . but here in the shade and breeze it is a trifle too cool.

"I was planning to drive to the seashore today but was persuaded to wait for the horses' sake till the cooler afternoon. I have a team and buggy out here from the Bagbys.

"Ma, strange to say, seems stronger this morning. Yet she takes absolutely no nourishment beyond perhaps a tablespoon of milk daily. She spoke to me this morning.

"The strawberries here continue to bloom and bear small quantities of fruit. The raspberries have not done well. Some of the grapes are doing well. Many of the others are dead. Oh, but it is so beautiful to look out over the yellow brown—the distant hills—the white and red cliffs toward Del Mar.

"This, I know, will be your favorite and future home and despite your protests I feel I should hasten its development for your sake and that of the children . . . . By sheer luck I believe that we have found here the most charming spot for a home in the most favored locality in the best part of the whole country . . . . "

A dictator's castle

With the 40-room Miramar house largely completed and orchards, dams and fields in place, EWS wrote to Ellen:

"I have closed one chapter in my life. My wife and children will hereafter treat my friends and guests as I wish them to be treated. All the old miserable embarrassments have ceased. I am running things now . . . . In a business way as in a domestic way I have declared myself dictator, emperor or any other old thing that means *I am running things myself now.*"

"Dear mistress"

Passionate about nature, EWS called Miramar "my own dear mistress," and "only solace," writing Bob Paine:

"As for myself I can say I have no tree so graceful, no cluster of bloom so beautiful as that which has formed my ideal while planting—that image I have painted on dream canvas.

"I line hours together, wandering over the ranch, staring at tree, bush, and humble vegetable, enjoying every view, but still more the images that I call up to observe what will be here . . . next week, next year . . . and 10 years after I am gone.

"Had I not been born of money-getting ancestors . . . I might have been happy and poor among green things and bright things, in love with sunrise and intoxicated by star twinkles. Come and take another look at my gardens, my groves, my mountains, my sea, and join me in cussing the Fate that forever keeps goading me on and away . . . . "

Boys manage ranch

April 8, 1901

To tie his sons closer to the land, Scripps hit on the idea of delegating each in turn at age 15 to be actual ranch manager, to hire and fire, handle money, make all decisions. A letter to Cleon Sweeney, Miramar foreman:

"The main idea is not to make money but to have a pleasant place to live . . . . I am trying to accustom Jim to being self-reliant but it is a little too early to start a boy out . . . . I want him to feel as my representative . . . . and taught to treat everybody properly . . . . The boys can do pretty much as they please . . . I would rather have one acre of beauty than fifty acres of yielding orchards."

DAMNED OLD CRANK

Not like fellow men

April 6, 1909

It did not matter to EWS that he wore the badge of crankiness. He considered the description benign. As he wrote on this date in a disquisition, *Damned Old Crank*:

"The word 'crank' is used to define the character of a man who does not think and act in the same way as the universality, almost, of his fellow man. I am fully entitled, I feel, to the name 'crank' and have no fault to being called an 'old crank,' and as I am almost universally judged to be peculiar, I am condemned as a crank. The word 'damned' means the same as condemned. Hence I am . . . 'a damned old crank'."

On wearing a full beard and stuffing his pants in his boots: "I wear a full beard when nearly everybody else shaves clean; to that extent I am willing to appear like a man and do not, like my fellows, make myself look like a girl."

[Because he tramped over rough ground, though brush and high grass, he wore boots.] "I am entirely free from the pest of fleas . . . (and) saved the annoyance of getting my shoes full of loose dirt, pebbles and sticky things in the grass and brush." [Ah, but why boots on city streets?] "My main and great reason is that protecting my ankles and the lower part of my legs from exposure to the cold air, I frequently avoid taking cold."

"... a business absurdity"

To Milton McRae:
"When I have been accused of slovenly habits, almost unintelligible chirography [handwriting] and uncouth and often disagreeable mannerisms, I have had only one self-satisfying consciousness; this is that it takes more time to keep one's self elegantly attired than any man of affairs can afford; that it takes more effort to write a copper-plate hand than it does to produce an able essay; and that politeness to all the world is a business absurdity and a physical as well as a mental impossibility."

EW did not suffer fools gladly. "I walk fast and drive my buggy on the run to save time. I never go to the church or theater ... to any social functions . . . [or] watch men play baseball or football ... hunt or play golf."

Private—Keep out!

October 4, 1898

To Ellen:
"My whole suite of rooms is not to be invaded by anyone but my wife and I intend to reserve one room where she will come to maintain her *right* without disturbing that solitude so dear, so desirable to me."

BACHELOR DAYS

A raging libido

1872-78

In his unpublished "History of The Scripps League," EWS candidly discusses the raging libido that tormented his bachelor days, asserting:

"I had a number of experiences . . . with actresses . . . Conditions being as they were, it was physically impossible for me to practice celibacy for more than a brief period of days."

"Oh, it is all pretty"

May 1, 1878

From Paris to Annie:

"Paris is a gay jolly city and like a bad young man as I am, I am seeing as much of the gaiety and jollity as I can . . . . But besides that, this is a beautiful city and full of beautiful things. Pictures superb by the mile, statues by the thousands, palaces grand and open to the public, churches so exquisitely beautiful as to be indescribable, parks without number filled with fountains and statuary, broad beautiful boulevards forever presenting the same holiday effect, beautiful women in carriages and on the street, theaters grand and concerts delightful. Cafes whose splendor outshines royal palaces . . . . Oh, it is all pretty, harmonious and enchanting. Paris is an intoxicating drink I love to quaff!"

Giving up Jessie

November 23, 1878

To Annie:

"I never cared enough for any woman to run the risk of hurting anyone's feelings by marrying her. I think it would be impossible for me to ever care enough for Jessie [Sweeney, his cousin], to want to marry her for a moment if I thought by doing so I would rob Fred [his brother] of the one great desire of his life."

His love for Lida

1881, St. Louis

Perhaps to cheer him up, Annie writes and asks for his "love story" and got graphic account of confusing courtship he carried on since age 16 to try to win cousin Lida Scripps:

"I never loved very hard. It is not in me to do that . . . . For 10 years I have determined to marry my cousin Lida. I have not played the lover much. I have talked and written to her more with the mein of giving her a thorough insight into my character than gaining her affections. I figure to win her at the cost of truth and honesty would be worse than a loss. She never cared much for me and the only food of hope I had was my great vanity.

"Finally I concluded from what she said in her last letter that she was tired of my suit. Then one day I was sick, just after the *Chronicle* had started, when I felt my business prospects were so bright and my heart and health prospects were so dull, I wrote her an insane letter, which she never answered.

"As for my feelings toward Lida, I can only say that she is the only woman I have ever known I would be willing to make my wife. It was not until I lost her entirely that I fully realized the strength of my feelings in regard to her. This [defeat] has probably affected my life more than anything else . . . I prepared myself by years of thought, labor and cultivation for this woman. The next one must take me as she finds me.

"I have let go another anchor, the only one in fact which controlled my life so far as purity or decency was concerned, and today I am completely adrift . . . . The only thing I have left now is my ambition and a certain kind of family affection . . . . My friends must leave me to pursue my own pleasures and my own mode of life. They must shut their eyes to its degradation or be satisfied with whatever other proofs of being worthy of esteem I give them.

"You may be surprised by my lame pursuit of an object so much desired and my tame submission to defeat. But you must understand that money and fame-hunting and love-making lead along widely diverging paths, and that failing health is a poor incentive for marriage . . . .

"I am not going whining through the rest of my life. I shall fight just as hard, laugh just as loud,

build air castles as high as I ever did . . . . I shall
study whether life is a tragedy or a farce. I have
never fully decided."

Quitting the fast life

His autobiography reveals a decision while
traveling abroad:

"I had come to the conclusion that a real,
lasting love affair was impossible for me. I had,
however, arrived at a condition of absolute disgust
for all those women who had light morals. I determined that when I put foot on American soil again
I would abandon drink and that I would abandon
companionship with loose women . . . . I determined
also to seek out some nice woman near my own
age—one to whom I could candidly acknowledge my
own past—marry her and rear a family of
children."

A quick courtship

July 3, 1882

To Annie:
". . . After my arrival home I shall be quite
content to marry the first girl who is decent, halfway intelligent, not inclined to ask for a longer

courtship than the few minutes necessary for me to make my proposition and receive an answer, and who can be depended upon not to bother me with too much of her personal attention after marriage."

". . . must have a family"

Having squired actresses and others of the demimonde in Detroit and kept a mistress in Cleveland, EWS from St. Louis wrote Annie that an unmarried man is always "more or less of a bummer and a rascal." He wanted to settle down, explaining:

"Of course I don't see the 'sin' of my present course, as you may, but then I feel somewhat the natural and necessary degradation and ostracism that it is gradually bringing me. I am not rich enough to defy public opinion and I am not hypocrite enough to attempt to deceive it.

"Then, too, I must have a family. I want to bring up carefully some children who will grow into young men and will become an honor to me and the family, which has always been weak in numbers of social and political influence. Am I not awfully practical? But I have been waiting so long for the overwhelming passion that I fear it is never coming.

"I am beginning to believe that I am what Bacon would call a great man. I have at least one of the elements which that philosopher associates to the class. He says that no great man ever truly loved a woman . . . . Now I am looking for a wife.

When I get her, I suppose you will all object . . . . I feel abundantly capable of making some nice, smart girl like me. I have done it before. But I don't want to start out in life by deceiving the woman I intend to marry. I don't want to play the silly heartsick lover, and then have her find out afterwards it was all show.

"And if I go to her and tell her I don't love her very much, but that I like her and respect her and want her to have me, she will be very indignant and send me about my business.

"In a woman's balance, namby-pamby weighs heavy while real respect and honor is light as a feather. I speak somewhat from experience. I like to experiment. But I don't think that I have ever yet thrown my fate into any woman's hands.

"I am going to do so as soon as I am satisfied that I shall not too bitterly repent if she takes me. And then if she doesn't—why, I'll draw a long breath and congratulate myself in having escaped a life connection with a person so weak-minded and silly as not to be able to appreciate a good thing when she saw it. Won't I be right?"

Catch whims on the fly

October 21, 1883

After his cousin Jessie Sweeney spurns his offer of marriage, EWS writes Annie:

"I don't understand much about young women of the orthodox school. Girls ought to make allowances for us old bachelors and catch our whims on the fly. Ought to know men in active and progressive lives have no time to waste in dawdling about with the ladies."

Falls for Minnie

February 18, 1884

Renting an apartment in a St. Louis dowager's mansion, EWS takes an interest in her 5-foot socialite daughter named Minnie, telling Ellen:

"I am living perfectly straight. I am getting all tangled up with my landlady's daughter. I moved out of one hotel here because the old landlord's young wife took to decorating my chamber with bouquets and three-cornered notes.

"So now I must either move out of my handsome apartment or give somebody else a legal right to share it . . . . I have half a mind to marry the girl and get out of this infernal business of debt and libel suits. She is good enough for me and under the circumstances would not feel entitled to make a slave of me.

"She lets me smoke in her parlor and does not read me temperance lectures every time she is reminded that I occasionally take a drink. She plays pretty well, and bosses the servants as I think they ought to be bossed. I guess she would kick if I gave her that ring and told her I got it for somebody else [his cousin Lida]."

Ought to be a monk

April 14, 1884

To Ellen, explaining his deepening involvement with Miss Minnie:

". . . For duty's sake I must run away from another woman who wants to be my wife. For duty's sake I ought to live the life of a monk. Here I am a man of 6 feet in stature, well enough proportioned, good enough looking in the face, with a finer mind than most men, capable of making myself both rich and famous, and yet with such a record for women.

"Robbed by courtesans, jilted by silly girls and having been pestered to death by the courtships or other love-making of a lot of silly fools whose only excuse is that I don't want to make love to them."

"What an idiot"

April 29, 1884

To Annie, in the same mood:

"My poor little love affair. What an idiot I was to think there was anything in the way of a woman that could give me more than passing interest . . . . I think of selling out and going out west to run a little sheep ranch."

A goofy proposal

EWS writes Ellen about his blunt proposal to Miss Minnie:

"What I says, says I to her, 'If you love me marry me and if you don't love me don't marry me. And I don't give a continental what you do only don't be so infernally skittish about it.' . . . I think I am a fool . . . . When I am with her I think I am dreadfully in love, but when I am away that is all right . . . . I wonder if most men don't lie to their wives and sweethearts just as I do to please them. I wonder if ladies don't tell the same kind of lies for the same purpose. I should not be surprised."

BLUES, FEUDS, ETC.

In the dumps in London

Spring, 1878

Caught in a rush-hour crowd on London Bridge, EWS describes terrible depression in his autobiography:

"The sight of so much humanity, the close contact with so much ugliness, misery, hopelessness, dull blankness of vision has oppressed me . . . I am just one of these . . . I felt a loathing for the whole species, including myself . . .

"I looked down at the water of the Thames . . . I yearned to throw myself over the parapet, and, in quick unconsciousness, accept the realization of what I was, and what all humanity was . . . . [Later] I was resolved to disassociate myself from the crowd, to climb up, and out, and over it . . . . if I were not to become a suicide."

'Puffs' for laughs only

Winter, 1878

In his autobiography:

"In 1878 it was the custom of the Cleveland daily papers to give every, even moderately large, advertiser a tremendous amount of 'puffs.' They would not only puff the merchant's business itself, but also the merchant and the merchant's wife and daughters.

"Every advertiser of the ordinary Cleveland newspaper could depend upon a good-sized notice in the reading columns of a birth of a baby in his family, or a death, or a marriage, or a social gathering at his home.

"*The Press* always refused to publish such items, or, if it published any notice at all of such events, it was generally with the object of ridicule, or at least to make the public laugh."

Work vs. caliber

May 20, 1880

Prior to start-up of *St. Louis Chronicle*, EWS wrangled about whether his cousin John Sweeney or his older half-brother George should be business manager. To Ellen:

"George has 10 times the mental and moral caliber that John has. But caliber is not what I want. I want work. Mean, nasty, disagreeable work. . . George's health will not permit him to do too hard work."

". . . riding a high horse"

To George:

"If you think I am big-headed and riding a high horse, why crack me on the head, and knock me off the horse, and come here yourself, or send anyone else you want. I am willing to clear out . . . There is too much mulishness in this firm."

"What more do you want?"

May 27, 1880

James scalded EWS, and ordered an "immediate halt" in planning for the new St. Louis paper, and the letter hit EWS, he confessed to Ellen, "like a clap of thunder, leaving me panic-stricken . . . . For the first five minutes . . . I felt like running, some wild thoughts of the far west."

To James:

"I was impatient of delay . . . my own incapacity to adjust to matters more quickly and satisfactorily . . . . I was desperate and wrote a foolish letter . . . . As for my judgment being 'only mediocre' . . . it has never been so weak as to lead me to disregard your instructions in the main . . . . I feel as yet unequal to the heavy load of a long continued responsibility.

"You should remember that I am only 26 years old and have had a very loose moral and mental training . . . . I am willing to stay here until your investment makes a handsome profit . . . . What more do you want?"

Cuffs for a cuss

May 28, 1880

To Ellen:
"The only thing that strikes me as unfortunate about the whole mess is that after knowing me so long George and James could find out for the first time that I am an arrogant, amusing, bombastic, champagne-drinking knave, and yet with all an amusing cuss . . . .

"Successful business relations could not exist between myself and James if I were to take the position he assigned me, viz: at his feet where I could have my feast made up of droppings of his wisdom and seasoned with kicks and cuffs . . ."

Hates 'mud-hole city'

December, 1880

Scripps, restless, bored, discouraged, grows to hate St. Louis, writing Annie:
". . . I am getting impatient to get away from this mud-hole city."

A pile of loose stones

January 21, 1881

The Scripps brothers pooled their newspaper holdings—with exception of *The Detroit News*—into a single unit called the Scripps Publishing Co. Even so, EWS and brother James continued to quarrel bitterly over business style. EWS writes Annie:

"The terror of my life has been a fear . . . I might fall [off his career ladder] and break my neck . . . I tremble now lest I have taken one step too many . . . . I am now standing at the top of a pile of very loose stones and if one of them slips, I'll come to the bottom a very bitter fellow."

". . . a degree of insanity"

February 17, 1881

To Ellen:

"The worry . . . has unsettled my mind somewhat, and I sometimes fancy that maybe my words and actions indicate even a degree of insanity. It must be that this is the case for I have never before experienced such difficulty as I am having in holding my own with my associates."

"A dagger . . . in my heart"

Back running *The Cleveland Press*, EWS prints a story inferring that Ed Cowles, publisher of the rival *News-Leader*, suffered problems in the roof of his mouth because of venereal disease. Cowles irately sued for libel. To Ellen:

"I am in for it again. It is disgusting. What am I going to do about it? Fight, just as hard and as long as my strength will hold out.

"There is no good minimizing matters. The case is a hard one . . . . I am as blue as ever a man was . . . . I feel as though a dagger was being stuck in my heart, and though I laugh, swagger, and boast, I feel tears starting in my eyes and I have to turn my head to hide them . . . . Now I feel like going off by myself and having a good cry . . . (but) I must stand up to the rack, bear the torture and grin and bear it . . . . I am going to prepare for battle and then lay myself out to do the biggest job of my life."

"False step"

To Ellen:
"I consider this the most serious false step of my journalistic career. I take an oath to extricate

myself from the concern in such a way as to win
some more respect for my ability in getting out
of the scrape than condemnation for getting into
it . . ."

"Darkest days"

May 4, 1881

Facing the Cowles libel trial, EWS broods, writing Ellen:

". . . Idleness is giving me lots of time to think. The result is I am thinking myself into a state of self-contempt and self-meanness never before experienced in my darkest days of morbidness. I feel I had rather be half-crazy with foolish thoughts than half-idiotic with liquor.

"My mental strength is just like a woman's smile. For the greatest part of the time it is weak and flabby. But at rare intervals, I feel like a giant!"

"Jesus freak factory"

January 26, 1885

Annie, crippled by arthitis, got taken in by a group of religious quacks that EWS called a "Jesus freak factory," and wrote him for money while he and Ellen were touring Cuba. He responded:

"You can have the money, but it makes me swearing mad that you are giving it to a pack of swindlers. If I were in Milwaukee I would put the law and the newspapers rooting out this pack of false pretenders as I did a set professing the same creed in Cincinnati a few months ago. We landed one of those rascals in prison . . . .

"It was such a plain worn-out swindle, that of offering you medical attendance for a dollar a mile and then roping you into a $200 lecture course . . . . If your friends are not murderers . . . instead of paying them $200 for their hoodoo business, offer them $1,000 for the slightest benefit—or nothing for no service rendered."

Dad's number

October 18, 1893

To Ellen:

"Jim [age 7] found me in my room smoking. 'Do you always smoke when you are mad at Mama, Dad?' I told him to get out. His parting shot was, 'I know you always drink when you are mad at Mama, or some of us are sick.' He has me sized up, and I can't fool him.

"I called him back and tried to convince him that the credit of his family depended on him not telling anybody such things."

A SUMMING UP

In a disquisition he titled "The Wisdom of Gatrox,", EWS came up with what he regarded as "quite good" advice for "my young friends" on how to get rich:

"If you had wanted to know how to become an alderman, a legislator, a congressman, a governor, a member of the President's cabinet, you should have gone to a politician.

"If you had wanted to know how to become a favorite with the ladies, you should have sought advice of Lothario.

"If you had wanted to become wise in philosophy and science, you should have gone to a college professor.

"There are many ways in which a man can become distinguished and there are a many kinds of men who can assist you in each of these ways as there are ways themselves.

"But you want to get rich. Very well, let's get down to brass tacks.

"*First.*—Never spend as much money as you earn. The smaller your expenditures are in proportion to your earnings the sooner you will become rich.

"*Second.*—It is more blessed to give wages than to accept them, or at least, it is more profitable.

"*Third.*—Never do anything yourself that you can get someone else to do for you. The more things that someone else does for you the more time and energy you have to do those things which no one else can do for you.

"*Fourth.*—Never do anything today that you can put off till tomorrow. There is always so much to do today that you should not waste your time and energy in doing anything today that can be put off until tomorrow. Most things that you do not have to do today are not worth doing at all.

"*Fifth.*—Always buy, never sell. If you've got enough horse sense to become rich, you know that it is better to run only one risk than two risks. You also know that just as likely as not the other fellow is smarter than you are and that whether you buy or sell, in each case you run the risk of getting the worst of the bargain. By adopting my rule you will diminish by one-half your chances of loss.

"*Sixth.*—Never do anything if you can help it that someone else is doing. Why compete with one person or many other persons in any occupation or line of business so long as it is possible for you to have a monopoly in some other field?

"*Seventh.*—If circumstances compel you to pursue some occupation or to follow some line of business, which occupation or line of business is being pursued by some other person or persons, then do you do your work in some other way than that in which it is done by others. There is always a good, better, and best way. If you take the best way, then the other fellow has no chance in competing with you.

"*Eighth.*—Whatever you do once, whatever way you undertake to do a thing once, don't do the same thing again or don't do the thing in the same way, because knowing one way of doing a thing you must know that there is a better way of doing the same thing.

"*Ninth.*—If you're succeeding in anything you are doing, don't let any one else know of your success, because if you do some other person or persons will try to do the same thing that you are doing and be your competitor.

"*Tenth.*—When you become rich, as you will become rich if you follow my advice, don't let any one know it. General knowledge of your wealth will only attract the tax-gatherer, and other hungry people will try to get away from you something they want and something you want to keep.

"*Eleventh.*—One of the greatest assets any man can secure is a reputation for eccentricity. If you have a reputation for eccentricity you can do a lot of things, you can even do the things you want to do without attaching to yourself the enmity of others. Many an act performed by an ordinary person which would arouse indignation, animosity, and antagonism can be performed by a man with a reputation of eccentricity with no other result than that of exciting mirth and perhaps pity and sympathy. It is better to have the goodwill than the bad will, even of a dog.

"*Twelfth.*—Never hate anybody. Hatred is a useless expenditure of mental and nervous energy. Revenge costs much of energy and gains nothing. Carlyle once said of the English people that there were so and so many millions of English people, mostly fools. When you find many people applauding you for what you do, and a few condemning, you can be certain that you are on the wrong course, because you're doing the things that fools approve of. When the crowd ridicules you and scorns you, you can know at least one thing, and that is that it is at least possible that you are acting wisely. It is one of the instincts of man to covet applause. The wise man regulates his conduct rather by reason than by instinct.

"*Thirteenth.*—It is far more important to learn what not to do than what to do. You can learn this invaluable lesson in two ways, the first of which and the most important is by your own mistakes, the second is by observing the mistakes of others. Any man that learns all the things that he ought not to do cannot help doing the things that he ought to do.

"*Fourteenth.*—Posterity never can do anything for you. Therefore, you should invest nothing in posterity. Of course, your heirs will quarrel over your estate, but that will be after you're dead, and why should you trouble your mind over things which you will never know anything about?

"*Fifteenth.*—A man can do anything he wants to do in this world, at least if he wants to do it bad enough. Therefore, I say that any of you who want to become rich can become rich if you live long enough.

"*Sixteenth.*—After what I have said, it goes without further saying that you should save money, but no man can save himself rich, he can only make himself rich. Savings are capital. It is only by doing things that one learns how to do things. It is only the capitalist who handles capital that learns how to handle capital profitably. The more capital you have the more skillful you become as a capitalist.

"*Seventeenth.*—Fools say that money makes money. I say that money does not make money, it is only men who make money.

"*Eighteenth.*—There are two cardinal sins in the economic world, one is giving something for nothing, and the other is getting something for nothing, and the greater sin of those two is that of getting something for nothing—or trying to do so. Really, I doubt if anyone ever does get something for nothing.

"Don't marry a rich wife. Women are what they are. At best they are hard enough to get along with. They are always trying to make a man do something that he doesn't want to do, and generally succeeding, but when a woman is conscious of the fact that she has furnished all or any part of your capital, her influence over you will be so great as to be the worst handicap that you can carry.

"*Nineteenth.*—If you're a prospective heir of

your father or some other relative, you should also consider that a handicap. I would advise you to refuse to be an heir.

"*Twentieth.*—Despise not the day of small things, but rather respect the small things. It is far easier to make a profit on a very small capital invested in any business than it is to make the same proportion of profit off of large capital. It is true that after you have learned how to make a profit on a business that has small capital, and after successively as your capital grows you learn how to handle it profitably, the time may come, aye, I would say that the greater your capital becomes in this way the greater your proportion of profits on it should be. And, for an additional reason, as your wealth and skill grow rapidly, your so-called necessary expenses grow much slower and in time cease to grow at all so that beyond a certain limit all your income and added income becomes a surplus, constantly to be added to your capital.

"*Twenty-first.*—It is far easier to make money than it is to spend money. As it becomes more and more difficult to spend money, you will spend less and less of it, and hence there will be more money to accumulate.

"*Twenty-second.*—The hardest of all labor performed by man is that of thinking. One can think hard and even think straight, and yet, without financial reward. If you have become rich, train your mind to hard thinking and hold it well in leash so that your thinking will all be with but one object in view, that of accumulating more wealth."

EWS

Career At-A-Glance

1854

June 18—Born on farm at Rushville, Ill.

1872

To Detroit to work with older half-brother James E., helps him start *The Detroit Evening News,* works mainly in circulation, finally taken on as cub reporter.

1877

Becomes city editor of *The Detroit Evening News.*

1878

Spring—Goes to Europe as traveling companion with older half-brother George.

November 2—With cousin John Sweeney and brothers James and George founds *Cleveland Penny Press.*

1880

July 31—Launches *St. Louis Chronicle* with his brothers.

1881

Returns to Europe with sister Ellen for year and a half of traveling.

1883

January 1—Acquires control of *Cincinnati Penny Paper*.

1890

Starts *The Kentucky Post,* creates Scripps-McRae League to run his papers; visits California and buys desert acreage and begins eight-year building of Miramar ranch.

1892

Acquires first Pacific Coast paper, *San Diego Sun.*

1895

Starts *Los Angeles Record.*

1896

Acquires *Kansas City World.*

1899

Starts *Seattle Star* and *Akron Press.*

1900-08

Starts or acquires 19 more papers; founds United Press and Newspaper Enterprise Association.

1908

"Retires" and turns reins over to son Jim, 22. Starts four new papers.

1917

EWS returns to duty when U.S. enters World

War I; because of policy differences, Jim breaks away five West Coast papers, and *Dallas Dispatch.*

November—Suffers stroke in Washington; recuperates on series of yachts, spending most of rest of his life at sea.

1920

Formally turns business over to son Robert and Roy W. Howard.

1920-24

Starts or acquires 11 newspapers, and changes name of concern to Scripps-Howard.

1926

March 12—Dies aboard yacht "Ohio" at Monrovia, Liberia.

March 14—Buried at sea, as per wish. [Latitude 6 degrees, 14 minutes, 0 seconds north, Longitude 11 degrees, 8 minutes, 0 seconds west.]